"Eye-opening, hilarious, and absolutely original, *Humor, Seriously* will change the way you think on the job, about the world, and in your life."

—LESLIE BLODGETT, founder and former CEO of Bare Escentuals

"Of all the known ways to ruin humor, the most common start with the words 'research,' 'analyze,' and 'professor.' The bad news is that this book features all of those words. Prominently. The good news is that against all odds, you'll actually have fun reading it. It probably won't turn you into Ali Wong, Dave Chappelle, or Hannah Gadsby, but it will give you a much deeper appreciation of how they think—and teach you some new ways to make people laugh."

—ADAM GRANT, *New York Times* bestselling author of *Originals* and *Give and Take*, and host of the TED podcast *WorkLife*

"In this eye-opening, important, and utterly enjoyable book, Jennifer Aaker and Naomi Bagdonas use science to explain how humor at work (and in life) helps alleviate stress, anxiety, and burnout. Come for the humor, stay for the insights."

—ARIANNA HUFFINGTON, co-founder of *The Huffington Post* and CEO of Thrive Global

"If this book and Brad Pitt walked into a bar, and I could only pick one, I'd take the book home with me."

—NANCY LUBLIN, former CEO, Crisis Text Line and DoSomething.org

"Jennifer Aaker and Naomi Bagdonas have written a remarkable book for a remarkable moment in history. I learned long ago that when weighed down by serious matters, one may best be taken seriously by seeking out a certain lightheartedness as an expression of humility, optimism, and confidence on the road to the serious business of nurturing trust and leading others."

—JOEL PETERSON, Chairman of JetBlue Airways

"Fresh, profound, and consistently entertaining. I know the words 'evidence-based' don't immediately connote riotous laughter, but Aaker and Bagdonas bring some irresistibly compelling science to the art and application of humor. "

—KELLY LEONARD, executive vice president of The Second City

HUMOR, SERIOUSLY

Humor,

Currency · New York

SERIOUSLY

WHY HUMOR IS A SECRET WEAPON
IN BUSINESS AND LIFE*

* AND HOW ANYONE CAN HARNESS IT. EVEN YOU.

JENNIFER AAKER

&

NAOMI BAGDONAS

Published in the United States by Currency, an imprint of Random House, a
division of Penguin Random House LLC, New York.

CURRENCY and its colophon are trademarks of Penguin Random House LLC.

LIBRARY OF CONGRESS CATALOGING-IN-PUBLICATION DATA

Names: Aaker, Jennifer Lynn, author. | Bagdonas, Naomi, author.
Title: Humor, seriously / Jennifer Aaker and Naomi Bagdonas.
Description: First edition. | New York : Currency, [2021] | Includes
bibliographical references and index.
Identifiers: LCCN 2020019332 (print) | LCCN 2020019333 (ebook) | ISBN
9780593135280 (hardcover) | ISBN 9780593238424 | ISBN 9780593135297 (ebook)
Subjects: LCSH: Wit and humor—Psychological aspects. | Laughter. |
Management—Psychological aspects. | Organizational behavior.
Classification: LCC BF575.L3 A25 2021 (print) | LCC BF575.L3 (ebook) |
DDC 152.4/3—dc23
LC record available at https://lccn.loc.gov/2020019332
LC ebook record available at https://lccn.loc.gov/2020019333

Printed in the United States of America on acid-free paper

randomhousebooks.com

2 4 6 8 9 7 5 3 1

First Edition

To our parents, grandparents, and Connor (who is neither).

*To Carla and Andy and the countless people who were
with us on this journey.*

*To those who do good and devote their lives to serving others.
To the present.*

*   *   *

*Look to this day!
For it is Life,
The very Life of Life.*

Humor Makes Us Human

By Ed Catmull

L et's talk about humor. But first, let's talk about stories.

The typical story has three acts that go something like this: The first act tells the audience what the problem is and why they should care. The second act is where it all goes wrong—so very, very wrong. The third act is where, unlike in real life, it all gets resolved. How exactly it ends, though, is, just like in real life, always a surprise.

In our Pixar movies, we searched for stories that had meaning, something that resonated with us personally, that emerged from our collective experiences, that illuminated the fun and games, adventures and heartbreaks. He wasn't just a rat—he was a courageous little rat with big dreams of becoming a world-class chef.

We found that the best way to connect that meaning to people on a fundamental and emotional level is to deliver it with humor.

In fact, it's pretty hard to make a point about deeper meaning without humor. It all becomes too on the nose, too obvious. It doesn't take; it's more like lecturing. And no one wants a lecture from a rat in a chef hat.

Humor isn't about jokes or arbitrariness—to resonate, it should arise naturally out of the characters themselves. The space and texture that creates humor within the narrative of a film, or the arc of a character, is what creates meaning for an audience.

That's the way life has to be as well.

We all want meaning in our lives. And yet, there are times when work and life get serious and hard, mundane and stressful. Having a sense of humor doesn't just punctuate and offset the seriousness— it allows the meaning to come through. Unexpected moments with co-workers, partners, families, and friends shake things up and keep you on your toes. They define the shape of your relationship as much as the hard moments do. Playfulness and bonding with one another in the good times are of tremendous value during the times when things get more serious.

This is true not just for us as individuals, but for us as leaders of organizations, too.

Pixar has faced many problems since its inception. Difficult, serious problems. Money problems, culture problems, losing fantastic team members who defined us . . . problems. In these moments, what I found was that *what* I said as a leader didn't matter—they were just words that washed away; what people grabbed on to was *how* I behaved. One has to admit failures and take actions that demonstrate real values.

Doing so with a healthy sense of humor—with the intellectual perspective, empathy, and humanity it brings—is a vital part of responding to the unexpected, of adapting to new realities. Words matter little; behavior and attitude are what count.

A sense of humor is part of what makes us human. It's a deeply connecting and empowering thing. Deploying it doesn't make light of serious things, it means you're able to move forward, in spite of those serious things.

And that's exactly what a good Pixar protagonist does in the third act. They adapt, they change, they fix the problem. In our movies, they do it with humor . . . and, sometimes, with a dash of paprika.

Where there is serious work punctuated by levity—that's where we find meaning.

Have a meaningful read,
Ed

CONTENTS

HUMOR, SERIOUSLY

Gravity

and Levity

"The law of levity is allowed to supersede the law of gravity."

—R. A. Lafferty

One crisp October evening in 2016, a group of ten behavioral scientists and lecturers stood on a stage in Chicago. We hailed from Stanford, Harvard, Columbia, and the University of Pennsylvania— a cast of characters who could (and probably do) lecture in their sleep on topics like human cognition, artificial intelligence and human well-being, global wealth distribution, negotiations, and decision making.

But we weren't onstage together that day to lecture (or sleep). We were there to perform sketch comedy.

Now, academics—like businesspeople—aren't known for being funny. (Or charismatic or fun or cuddly . . . we get it.) Yet the ten of us had convened for a two-day humor summit at the world-famous comedy theater and training center The Second City, because the research to date couldn't be more clear: Humor has a profound impact on human psychology and behavior. And we believed that this emerging field just might become one of the greatest competitive advantages in business. Seriously.

Over those two days, we discussed past work done in the field and brainstormed new areas of interest that would define our future research together. The questions ranged from the broad and lofty, like how humor influences power, trust, and creativity, to the tactical, like how to craft a joke. Also we threw an imaginary purple ball around and yelled things like "Blerg!" and "Zippity zoop!" You know, in the name of science.

We got a crash course in humor techniques from Second City comedy experts Anne Libera and Kelly Leonard, who had trained talents like Stephen Colbert, Steve Carell, and even some talents not named Steve, like Tina Fey, Chris Redd, and Julia Louis-Dreyfus. All of which culminated in an exhilarating onstage sketch comedy performance.

The summit kicked off a multiyear exploration confirming the hypothesis that brought us all to the stage that day: From a research perspective, humor is serious business. And it's vastly underleveraged in most workplaces today.

For some, this stems from a fundamental misunderstanding about humor's benefits: the belief that gravity and levity are at odds. But the research tells a different story. That in fact, when we refuse to take ourselves so seriously, we relieve the stress standing in the way of serious work, create more meaningful connections with our colleagues, and open our minds to more innovative solutions.

For others, they understand at least some aspects of humor's power intuitively, but when it comes to harnessing it with intention, few know how.

This is a serious problem. Beyond leaving a whole lot of benefit on the table, this lack of levity in our work lives has dire consequences for our physical health (our workplaces are killing us), our relationships (the single greatest driver of happiness at a time when we are growing more disconnected than ever), and our teams and our companies (which are struggling to compete in a rapidly transforming world). We also suspect that it contributes to a permanent and unsightly frown known as "resting boss face."

We wrote this book to set the record straight, to unpack the benefits of humor for our careers, our businesses, and our lives using the sexiest means known to academics: behavioral science (plus a lot of help from comedians and business leaders). In it, you'll learn why humor is so powerful, why it's underutilized, and—most important—how *you* can use more of it, better.

Yes, you. Our favorite reader. The hero of this book.

But enough about you.

About Us

We have spent the last five years living and breathing the study of humor: Jennifer, as a behavioral scientist and chaired professor at Stanford who studies how meaning and purpose shape the choices individuals make. And Naomi, as an executive coach to leaders and celebrities, who has spent the last decade straddling corporate strategy and comedy.

We are also the creators (and teachers) of a course called "Humor: Serious Business" at Stanford's Graduate School of Business, where we teach some of the world's most ambitious, smart, and caffeine-addled business minds how to use humor and levity to transform their future organizations and lives. Our MBA students get the same amount of academic credit for our course about the power of humor as they do for "Managerial Accounting" and "Financial Trading Strategies."

Now, that's funny. Also: serious business.

But how did we get there? For Naomi, it started with an offhand comment from a client:

"I bet I know exactly what you do on Friday nights, Naomi."

An odd remark from someone who'd hired her as a consultant, but Bonnie and Naomi had grown close over the last three months. As a strategy consultant, Naomi oversaw the team helping Bonnie's organization redefine their customer experience. The project was intense, and she and Bonnie had spent hundreds of hours working together.

Bonnie continued, in all sincerity, to describe her vision of Naomi's Friday night. It involved Naomi "re-ironing her blouses for the next week" in a gray-walled apartment with landscape paintings and a cat. When pressed, she guessed the cat was named "Cat."

Oof.

In an instant, Bonnie had held up a mirror revealing Naomi's work self—and the reflection was disheartening in its inauthenticity: someone polished and austere and irrefutably good at her job, but utterly bereft of the joy and personality that made her *her*.

What's more, Bonnie's assessment wasn't off base; Naomi had been leading a double life. And not the steamy kind with fast cars and fancy hotels; no one at work knew that Naomi studied and performed comedy by night, and none of her comedian friends knew she advised Fortune 50 clients by day. For years, she kept these pursuits carefully siloed—after all, neither screamed "transferable skills" to the other.

But upon closer inspection, Naomi saw the incredible power of humor outside of comedy—how it had shaped her most meaningful friendships defused tense moments, prompted perspective and empathy, persuaded people to act, and bolstered resilience, especially in hard times. All while making things a whole lot more enjoyable.

After the experience with Bonnie, Naomi set out to prove that she could have more joy at the office and make humor an asset at work—and that she could help her clients do the same.

Jennifer had no time for that shit.

For her, humor was never a focus. Sure, she liked laughter (note: it's impossible to write that sentence without sounding like a sociopath), but was far more interested in research, writing, and getting work done.

That view fundamentally changed for her in 2010, when she wrote a book, *The Dragonfly Effect*, with her husband—about the power of story and networks to drive positive change in the world. During the first year following the book's launch, she worked with a Stanford student group called 100K Cheeks, applying the tools from the book toward the goal of getting over 100,000 new people into the national bone marrow registry.

That was when she met Amit Gupta, one of the seventeen patients she worked with. Amit had been diagnosed with leukemia and needed a bone marrow transplant, but no one registered with the National Marrow Donor Program was a perfect match. And so, he and his friends set out to reach as many South Asians as possible and persuade them to register with the donor bank.

Though Amit was mired in one of the most objectively somber corners of the human experience, Jennifer saw how he—and his friends, family members and colleagues—somehow managed to infuse humor and levity into every nook and cranny of his campaign.

On his website (AmitGuptaNeedsYou.com), visitors were greeted by him sporting a goofy red T-shirt and equally goofy smile. "Bone marrow donations are done with a process similar to blood donations. It's painless, but boring." He posted lighthearted messages about his search for a donor on Twitter and Tumblr, and hosted in-home bone marrow events at which he joked that guests should "BYOSA: bring your own South Asian" and "swab parties" at trendy NYC bars. And he teamed up with DoSomething.org to enlist comedians for the campaign—like a lighthearted (but heartfelt) PSA with Aziz Ansari and Chris Pratt urging students to "give a spit about cancer."

It worked. On January 20th, 2012, Amit found a perfect match.

While confronting his own mortality, Amit cultivated levity, which made him and everyone around him more motivated, nimble, and effective at getting people to register. After watching Amit persist, rally, and ultimately survive this deadly blood disease, Jennifer realized that humor could drive people in ways she had never before imagined.

* * *

Through these experiences, we realized we'd sorely underestimated humor's potential to transform work and life. So we set out to look at both.

Naomi dove more fully into the study of comedy—moving to LA to learn from her comedic heroes and train at the Upright Citizens

Brigade Theatre, while integrating principles of comedy into her coaching work with executives.

And Jennifer turned to research, specifically the behavioral science of humor, how it works to influence people's motivation, decision-making, and emotional and physical health—and how it might be harnessed to scale meaningful impact in the world. All while (non-sociopathically) laughing.

But the real magic—the David Copperfield, fireworks-worthy, make-the-Statue-of-Liberty-disappear stuff—would start when we brought these worlds together.

The two of us met in 2014, after Jennifer invited Naomi to guest lecture in her "Power of Story" class on a completely unrelated topic: how to effectively blend story with data.

Watching the students react to Naomi delivering her content, Jennifer was astonished to see that they were laughing—hysterically—while learning about neurochemical brain systems and factor analysis.

This fact bears repeating: They were laughing while learning about neuroscience and statistical methods. What's more, Jennifer observed that the students applied Naomi's concepts over the course of the semester and remembered them vividly eight weeks later.

When we hopped on the phone to debrief after the quarter was over, the call digressed from a simple recap into a passion-fueled exploration of the questions that would inevitably lead us here, with you: What if, together, we could blend the behavioral science of humor with principles from comedy, and apply them in a way that would actually be useful in business? Could this deepen relationships, make people more effective and joyful at work, and fundamentally transform companies—and maybe even the world?

And so we sharpened our quills and began to write. This book is our attempt to answer those questions.

What We've Been Up To

Over the past six years, our partnership has included conducting a dizzying amount of research, running experiments in the real world, and building a beautiful friendship along the way.* Specifically:

We ran studies involving over 1.5 million people across 166 countries with the goal of understanding things like how and why humor works (or fails), how humor differs over one's lifespan and across cultures, the nuanced relationship between humor and status, and particularly how the self-proclaimed unfunny becomes (less un)funny.

We pored through empirical research in psychology (e.g., decision-making and motivation), sociology (e.g., social movements and narrative identity), and neuroscience and biology (e.g., brain chemistry and physiology of laughter). And then we pored over some more research, just for a treat.

We trained with some of the best comedy institutions in the world, from sketch comedy with The Second City to improvisational comedy with the Upright Citizens Brigade and the Groundlings Theater. We spent hundreds of hours practicing and then performing in dimly lit improv theaters and experienced firsthand what it feels like to bomb, again and again. And then, slowly, to get better.

---

* Which one of our students described in a course evaluation as "uncomfortably close."

We jet-setted* across the country to meet real-life comedians who shared their wisdom and secrets. We talked to Norman Lear about the power of humor to tap a cultural vein, interviewed *The Onion* founder Scott Dikkers about his creative process, and asked comedian Sarah Cooper about the inspiration for her lip sync videos. We cornered Jimmy Fallon in the backstage hallway of *The Tonight Show* and sent perfectly sharpened pencils to Seth Meyers because he once mentioned, under his breath, barely audibly, that he likes them. Our process was academic and charming and not at all stalky.

We interviewed hundreds of leaders across industries. We talked to CEOs of companies ranging from tech giants like Twitter and Google to venture capital firms like Andreessen Horowitz to creative consultancies like IDEO to comedy machines like *Funny or Die* and *Saturday Night Live*. We interviewed political leaders like former U.S. secretary of state Madeleine Albright about how humor helped her in diplomacy and negotiations when the stakes were high.

We spent an hour playing fetch with a very friendly dog, just to catch a break.

We consumed a boatload of comedy. Naomi spent hundreds of hours going to improv and stand-up shows *by herself* because she couldn't make friends fast enough to sustain her ~~addiction~~ research. Jennifer watched every episode of *SNL* since 1975, made Trevor Noah's *Born a Crime* mandatory reading for all her kids (and students, but they signed up for it), and watched John Mulaney's *Come-*

---

*This just means we flew. In coach.

back Kid so many times that his lines now seep out of her mouth frequently and involuntarily.

Then we stress-tested our ideas to ensure they held up.

We ran workshops at companies like McKinsey, Deloitte, and Forrester. And also a bunch of companies that don't do consulting, but the point is that if management consultants can learn to leverage humor, then there is hope for us all.

We incorporated these principles into talks and coaching with executives and celebrities, from the sets of *The Tonight Show* and *Saturday Night Live* to company all-hands meetings to political campaign speeches to talks delivered at United Nations convenings.

We taught courses with hundreds of Stanford MBAs and executives, who have put our principles into action in ways that exceed our wildest dreams—a serial entrepreneur who created a company manifesto leavened with humor, an engineer who built an art installation to visualize the cultural nuances of humor, a food scientist who proposed to her (then) boyfriend* by creating a comic book of their lives together, and more.

At every turn, our findings challenged the false dichotomy between gravity and levity and uncovered the profound benefits of a life fueled by levity. If there's one thing our research makes clear, it's that we don't need to take ourselves so seriously in order to grapple with serious things.

---

* A story involving a "then boyfriend" implies an ending that could go one of two ways. In this case, it was the happy way.

The balance of gravity and levity gives power to both.
Which is, of course, why we're all here.

The Game Plan

If you're anything like the business people we know, you probably love game plans. And road maps. And road maps to navigate game plans. (Maybe a playbook?) So here's what you can expect to find in the chapters ahead.

The humor cliff (*chapter 1*). Before we can learn how to use humor more effectively at work, we need to understand what's holding us back. We'll debunk four of the most common myths about humor at work, and share an important framework for understanding the relationship between levity, humor, and comedy. Then we'll explore four distinct styles of humor and help you identify yours. Because who doesn't love a good typology?

Your brain on humor (*chapter 2*). We'll dig into the science: how our brains are hardwired to respond to humor and laughter, and how humor has been proven in the behavioral research to (among other things) increase perceptions of status, quicken the path to meaningful connection, unlock creativity and innovation, and boost resilience.

The anatomy of funny (*chapter 3*). Next, we'll delve into the world of comedy, understanding what makes something funny, training our brains to look at the world through a different lens, and crafting humor using the techniques of professional comedians.

How we lost 40 lbs with humor (and you can, too!). We're kidding. Chapter 4 has nothing to do with this.

Putting your funny to work (*chapter 4*). Maybe you intuitively understand the power of humor and have plenty of it in your "real" life but struggle to incorporate it at the office. We'll share a set of simple strategies to help you start using more of it—strategically—in your day-to-day work.

Leading with humor (*chapter 5*). As anyone who has climbed the ranks of an organization knows, status changes the game in many ways. We'll explore why humor is a powerful leadership strategy, and we'll build on the tools we've spent the previous chapters exploring to show how some of the most remarkable and effective leaders harness humor to enhance their power—while garnering the trust of those they lead. Because after all, in the wise and sassy words of the leadership guru John Maxwell: "If you're leading and no one is following, you're just taking a walk."

Creating a culture of levity (*chapter 6*). Organizational cultures (like empires and babies) aren't created by one person alone. Far more powerful than any one leader's harnessing humor is creating the conditions in which humor can come from anywhere. We'll show how a culture of levity helps teams and organizations thrive, and how you can start transforming your own culture in small but meaningful ways.

Navigating the gray areas of humor (*chapter 7*). What people find funny—and appropriate—is far from universal, and no one nails it every time. We'll explore why humor fails happen and what to do about them, giving you tools to recognize your gaffe, diagnose the situation, and make it right when you do accidentally cross a line. Also, we'll remind you not to be an asshole.

Why humor is a secret weapon in life (*chapter 7.5*). Don't get us wrong: we care about you becoming a badass business titan. But we care more about you as a whole person, and the opportunity for you to use the concepts in this book to live a better, more fulfilling life. We'll explore why the lessons from this book extend far beyond your workday.

Encore

At the end of the two-day summit at The Second City, the two of us packed up our things (imaginary purple balls and all), bade adieu to our collaborators / fellow performers, and parted ways at O'Hare Airport. As Naomi walked to her gate, the most unexceptional thing happened.

She went to buy an apple from an airport bodega.

As she approached the woman behind the register, she asked if the apples stacked in a gorgeous, waxy pyramid display were for sale. To which the woman looked Naomi up and down and curtly replied: "If you want one, get in line." So Naomi got in line, and watched as the cashier continued snapping at one customer after another. Impatient. Terse. Tarter than the Gala apples stacked before her.

When it was Naomi's turn, she could simply have said, "I'll have an apple." But after her weeklong full-body immersion in the world of comedy, she saw an opportunity to introduce a spark of levity into the interaction.

"Can I please have your *favorite* apple?" she said with a smile.

The woman paused, confused. "My favorite?"

"Yes. Your absolute favorite."

Then, a smirk. On a dime, everything shifted. The woman began digging through the pile of apples, laughing at first to herself and then with Naomi as they meticulously inspected each. When Naomi went to pay, the woman replied, still smiling, "Don't worry about it. I don't charge for my favorite apple."

More than anything, this book is about finding your apple moments. You'll learn tools for bringing humor into big, important moments, but also the little ones in between. Whether you're pitching an idea to your team or buying fruit from an airport bodega—a hint of levity has the power to transform an interaction, forge a connection, and signal that you see the other person. By understanding the science, mechanics, and applications of humor (in our brains, in our businesses, and in our lives), we can shift the way we look at the world—and the way it looks back at us.

Let's do this.

CHAPTER 1

The

Humor Cliff

"Humor is mankind's greatest blessing."

—*Mark Twain*

It's the first day of spring quarter at Stanford's Graduate School of Business. Fifty students excitedly file into a lecture hall, a few still wondering whether the course they've registered for is an elaborate joke played by the administration. "Humor: Serious Business" is about to begin.

Whiteboards line the walls; all the chairs and tables have wheels, for easy rearranging. It's a setting that's ideal for workshopping and terrible for napping. Jennifer, in her self-appointed role as DJ, has David Bowie's "Rebel Rebel" blasting. Naomi has a clip from *SNL* cued up to kick off the lecture.

And yet trepidation hangs heavy in the air.

Before class begins each semester, we have our students complete a "Humor Audit," a self-reflection exercise / terrifyingly personal quiz about how they use humor in their lives.* It includes questions like "Who or what makes you laugh the most in your life?" and "Who do you feel the funniest around?" and "Please submit complete documentation of your income, expenses, and assets for the previous fiscal year."†

So it's understandable that the students feel spooked: A sense of humor is like a muscle—it atrophies without regular use. Unfortunately, we find that in most students and executives we start working with, atrophy abounds. Just look at these responses to the question "When was the last time you really laughed?":

---

*Note: this is the most enjoyable kind of audit, because it focuses on what you find funny and not on tax evasion. (Unless you find that funny.)

†Surprise! This was an IRS audit all along.

"I honestly can't remember. Is that terrible?"

"I've been thinking and am drawing a blank! I know I laugh. Or at least I thought I did, which now I'm questioning . . ."

"On Tuesday, I did not laugh once. Not once. Who knew a class about humor could be so depressing?"

The good and bad news about these responses is that our students are not alone. And it's not Tuesday.*

The Humor Cliff

The collective loss of our sense of humor is a serious problem afflicting people and organizations globally. We're all going over the humor cliff together, tumbling down into the abyss of solemnity below.

At the bottom of that abyss we're joined by the majority of 1.4 million survey respondents in 166 countries who revealed in this Gallup poll that the frequency with which we laugh or smile each day starts to plummet around age twenty-three.

Global Humor Cliff

(Gallup data 2013 n = 1.4 million)

Y-axis: % of people who reported smiling / laughing a lot yesterday
X-axis: Participant Age

---

* We had a 6 in 7 shot of being right on this and took the swing.

To some extent, this pattern makes sense. As kids, we laugh all the time. The average four-year-old laughs as many as three hundred times per day. (The average forty-year-old, by comparison, laughs three hundred times every two and a half months.) Then we grow up, enter the workforce, and suddenly become "serious and important people," trading laughter for ties and pantsuits.

Before long, we lose levity entirely in a sea of bottom lines, slide decks, and mind-numbing conference calls. Our sense of play is repressed by a dizzyingly complex and dynamic professional environment, full of social land mines that are difficult to gauge and feel safer to avoid. As a result, most of us choose to keep our interactions sterile, measured, and professional; we go to work each day and leave our sense of humor—and so much more of ourselves—at the door.

This response signals a fundamental misunderstanding about how to work—how to solve important problems, how to conduct ourselves, and how to be successful.

We don't need more "professionalism" in our workplaces. Instead, we need more of ourselves, and more *human* connection—especially as in-person meetings are replaced by video chats and more relationships are sustained entirely by email. Often, all it takes is a hint of levity to shift a moment, or a relationship, from transactional and robotic to relational and authentic.

So what's holding us back?

Our research reveals four common misperceptions—or, as we like to call them:

The Four Deadly Humor Myths*

After we surveyed more than seven hundred people across a wide range of industries and levels about what holds them back from using humor at work, four themes emerged, each rooted in a myth that needs debunking. It's *MythBusters, Business Edition*.

THE SERIOUS BUSINESS MYTH

A large portion of our respondents reported **believing that humor simply has no place amid serious work.**

Early in our careers, this myth often stems from insecurity about our lack of experience. (This is before we're experienced enough to know nobody really knows anything.) We worry about harming our credibility and not being taken seriously.

Yet according to surveys of hundreds of executive leaders conducted by Robert Half International and Hodge-Cronin & Associates, 98 percent reported preferring employees with a sense of humor, while 84 percent believed employees with a sense of humor do better work. And humor affects not just how our leaders perceive us, but also how our peers do: Showing our sense of humor can make our peers more likely to attribute higher status to us and to vote us into leadership roles.

As we rise through the ranks in our careers, this misconception evolves. With greater status comes greater scrutiny; when we find ourselves on progressively bigger stages, we feel pressure to signal

---

* We read once that if you insert the word "deadly" in a title, people will be more likely to (a) read the subsequent content and (b) take it more seriously. Also, Nelson Cowan, the author of *The Magical Mystery Four: How Is Working Memory Capacity Limited, and Why?* calls the number four "magical" and a "mystery." Which is why we were all the more delighted to uncover four myths. Note: Cowan's book would have been even more popular had he not forgotten to include the word "deadly" in the title.

even more professionalism and "seriousness" to shareholders, customers, and colleagues. What's more, leaders report that the status differential makes it harder to show up as their authentic selves while also fulfilling the responsibilities of their public role.

But now more than ever, they need to do both.

Today's leaders are facing a crisis of trust; nearly half of employees cite their lack of trust in leadership as the single biggest issue impacting their work performance.

What's more, when employees are asked what characteristics inspire trust in a leader, the responses that rise to the top—like "knowing the obstacles the leader overcame" and "speaks like a regular person"—tell a consistent story: Today's employees yearn for more authentic, human leaders. Aspirational, yes, but also flawed. Humor is a powerful leadership strategy to humanize oneself to employees, break down barriers, and balance authority with approachability. (So powerful in fact that we wrote an entire chapter about it—damn.) As one example, leaders who use self-deprecating humor are rated higher on measures of both trustworthiness and leadership ability by their employees. While the bosses in question would probably downplay those gains with self-deprecating humor, they're very real.

And beyond the signals we send to our employees, a culture that balances serious work with levity and play can actually improve team performance. In a study involving more than fifty teams, researchers analyzed prerecorded team meetings as well as supervisors' ratings of team performance, both immediately and again two years later. The presence of humor in team interactions predicted more functional communication and higher team performance both in the moment and over time. Playful cultures allow teams to thrive, even (and especially) when the stakes are high and the times are hard.

Of course, we shouldn't go for funny *all* the time—that would be exhausting (and counterproductive). But we've swung so far in the other direction that our businesses thirst for it. The secret to success for many of the brilliant executives featured in this book is their ability to strike a delicate balance between gravity and levity; much like hot fudge and ice cream, each enhances the other. And both make something (your business prospects and glycemic index, respectively) rise precipitously.*

LEVITY CREATES BALANCE

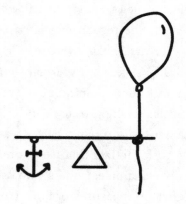

And if that adorable balloon *heroically balancing an anchor* isn't convincing enough, then let's pass the mic to President Eisenhower, who once said "A sense of humor is part of the art of leadership, of getting along with people, of getting things done."

If Dwight David Eisenhower, the second-least naturally funny president after Franklin Pierce, thought humor was necessary to win wars, build highways, and warn against the military-industrial complex, then you better learn to use it, too.

---

*Of note: beware the difference between analogy and equivalence. Just because something is like hot fudge and ice cream doesn't mean it's a substitute. Try telling your kids they can have a balance of gravity and levity for dessert, and see how they react.

THE FAILURE MYTH

We wish we had a dollar for every time we've heard a student or client express **a deep, paralyzing fear that their humor will fail.***

They're terrified of the awkward silence following a joke that falls flat, or, worse, the ensuing revelation that they've unintentionally offended someone.

But research shows that we get failure wrong. Not all humor "fails" are created equal, and every time you get a laugh is not necessarily a "win."

Over the last several years, three of our partners in crime from the Second City retreat—Brad Bitterly, Maurice Schweitzer, and Alison Wood Brooks—have run a series of experiments at Wharton and Harvard exploring humor's impact on perceptions of status, competence, and confidence—and, just as important, the impact of failed humor on each.

In one experiment, subjects were asked to read a transcript of a job interviewee's response to the question "Where do you see yourself in five years?" Some of the responses were serious, while others were tongue-in-cheek (e.g., "celebrating the fifth anniversary of your asking me this question"). Subjects were then asked to rate the interviewees on competence, confidence, and status.

The results weren't what you might expect. It turned out that the most important determinant of whether an interviewee was viewed more positively or negatively was not whether their response elicited laughter, but whether it was perceived as *appropriate*. In other words, it's not so much whether you're actually funny—it's whether you have the gumption to tell *any* joke (which signals con-

---

*Technically, we do get at least a dollar every time a student expresses this fear, since we are paid more than a dollar per student, though we don't let them express this fear more than once.

fidence), and whether that joke is appropriate for the context, that
signals status and competence.

This chart sums it up pretty well:

The upper right quadrant is still the sweet spot you'd expect it
to be—increasing perceptions across all three factors: confidence,
competence, *and* status. **Jackpot!**

The left half of the chart, according to our trusty laughter barometer, is what we typically tend to think of as failure: that is,
nobody laughed. But if you find yourself in the upper left quadrant,
you're **still good!** Even humor that people don't find laugh-out-
loud funny still leaves us better off if it's regarded as *appropriate*—
increasing others' perceptions of our confidence and having no
meaningful impact on status or competence.*

The lower half of the chart is how we define failure—humor

---

*In cases where a joke's appropriateness is ambiguous, a lack of laughter can
cause people to view the joke as less appropriate as well, which can result in
a loss of status. This is why we always carry a laugh track for our deepest-cut
dad jokes.

that people find inappropriate, *whether or not it gets laughs*. Falling into these quadrants (the asshole and villain zone) tends to decrease perceptions of status and competence.

Of course, rarely do people intend to be villains or assholes—the lower quadrants of the graph aren't places we navigate to on purpose. But inadvertently crossing a line happens to the best of us and is a real risk, especially for those in highly visible or public positions. Throughout the book, we'll provide tools to mitigate these risks, avoid common pitfalls, and recover (and learn) from fails when they happen.

For now, though, let's just focus on redefining "failure" when it comes to humor. And by the end of the book, you'll be better at creating *real* humor wins and avoiding the fails that actually matter.

THE BEING FUNNY MYTH

Now we come to one of the trickiest myths: that **in order to use humor and levity in the workplace, you have to "be funny."** Seems logical, right? But believe it or not, what's far more important than "being funny" is simply signaling that you have a sense of humor.

Even if you're not comfortable being funny yourself, as long as you understand the value of humor at work, you can benefit from it. The mere act of signaling that your sense of humor has a heartbeat is enough to make a big difference—especially if you're in a leadership role. One study by researcher Wayne Decker found that managers *with a sense of humor* (regardless of whether they themselves were funny) were rated by subordinates as 23 percent more respected, 25 percent more pleasant to work with, and 17 percent friendlier.

So how exactly do you signal you have a sense of humor? Sometimes, it's as simple as laughing at others' jokes, or jumping on opportunities to lighten the mood. Even a friendly smile can work wonders. As former Twitter CEO Dick Costolo puts it, "You don't have to be the quickest wit in the room. The easiest way to have more humor at work is not to try to be funny—instead, just look for moments to laugh."

The good news is that if you're anything like these 174,000 Gallup respondents, you're likely doing this a lot more outside the office already. On average, the data shows, we tend to smile and laugh much more on the weekends than on weekdays.

So you've been practicing:

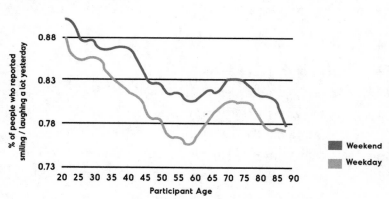

Humor Cliff, Weekend Edition
(Gallup data 2013 n = 174,000)

Keep in mind, the vast majority of business cultures span the spectrum from painfully boring to soul-crushingly serious. And it's more often a bit of fun rather than full-on funny that makes all the difference: a moment of delight that leads to a smile, or an "aha" rather than a "haha" (or, if you work for a supervillain, a "mwahaha").

THE BORN WITH IT MYTH
Comedians need both talent and training to succeed. But too many people are under the impression that **humor is an innate ability, not a skill you can learn.**

In other words, we tend to believe we're either funny or we're not; as researcher Carol Dweck would put it, we have a *fixed mindset*. However, thanks to the work of Dweck and her colleagues, we now know that a number of domains once thought to be wired into our genetic coding, like intelligence and creativity, are *not* fixed. We can change them by adopting what she calls a *growth mindset*. Humor is not some binary feature of our genetic code, but rather a skill we can strengthen through training and use, much as we would strengthen our leg muscles by working out at the gym, climbing stairs, and walking to and from the fridge during videoconferences when our "camera isn't working."

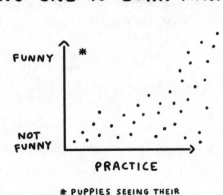

NO ONE IS BORN FUNNY*

FUNNY
NOT FUNNY
PRACTICE

* PUPPIES SEEING THEIR
REFLECTION FOR THE FIRST TIME

If you need proof that humor can be learned, travel back with us five years to when Jennifer was unanimously voted the least funny member of her family. Jennifer and her family were at home, enjoying a lovely dinner of Round Table pizza ("cooking," as she calls it). Fresh into her research about the science of humor—and always on the lookout for new "data"—she decided to conduct a family poll. Subjects included her husband (Andy), two sons (Cooper and Devon), and daughter (Téa Sloane).

The question posed at the table was "Who is the funniest member of our family?"

No sooner had the words escaped her mouth than all three kids' eyes shot down, laser-focused on their vegetables. Andy batted at an invisible fly. Jennifer leaned in expectantly.

It was Téa Sloane—the youngest and bravest of the bunch*—who finally broke the silence. "Dad is the funniest in our family! Then comes us." She paused, looking around the table to see if she was forgetting anyone. "Also, our dog, Mackey. Then you."

The rest of them nodded, quietly but firmly, in a way that suggested Jennifer's place in the family humor hierarchy was as immovable as it was self-evident.

And now, five years later—fueled by a deep desire for global impact and familial redemption—Jennifer is the triumphant author of a book about humor. Proof that there is hope for you, too.

What's My Humor Style?

Not everyone is funny in the same way. Over the last six years, we've run a series of studies to tease apart individual differences in both *what* people tend to joke about and *how* they most naturally deliver their humor. Those studies have yielded four primary humor styles: the **Stand-up**, the **Sweetheart**, the **Magnet**, and the **Sniper**.

Understanding your natural humor style will allow you to wield it with precision and presence. Reading through the following descriptions should give you a sense for which one(s) resonate; for a more thorough assessment, head to humorseriously.com and take

---

*Dear Coop and Dev—this is untrue; you are all equally brave, and equally wonderful, and equally loved. But in this moment, Téa Sloane was the most candid, which sometimes counts as brave.

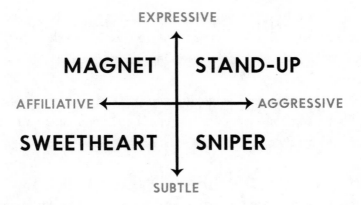

the Humor Styles Questionnaire or check out the mini quiz on page 237.

THE HUMOR STYLES

First, like any good lumberjack, let's understand our axes. The horizontal axis relates to the content of one's humor, from *affiliative* (wholesome, uplifting humor) to *aggressive* (humor that's no-holds-barred and a few shades darker).* The vertical axis measures delivery, from *expressive* (spirited, spontaneous, spotlight-seeking) to *subtle* (understated, premeditated, and full of nuance).

The Stand-up (Aggressive-Expressive)

Stand-ups are natural entertainers who aren't afraid to ruffle a few feathers to get a laugh. They come alive in front of crowds, and in group situations are almost always the ones cracking jokes. Stand-Ups believe that few topics are off-limits to joke about, and they

---

*This axis is inspired by the groundbreaking work of Rod Martin and Patricia Doris, though the specifics in how we define the axis differ from theirs. Note that Martin and Doris were conducting scientific research and writing academic articles on the topic of humor long before it was cool. Like it is now.

don't shy away from cursing, dark humor, pranks, and spontaneous roasts. Their thick skin means they can take it as well as they dish it out, and in fact they often see being the butt of a joke as a sign of affection.

If the world is your stage and you don't mind sacrificing some dignity (or someone's feelings) to get a laugh, you might lean toward the Stand-up style.

The Sweetheart (Affiliative-Subtle)

Sweethearts are earnest and honest, and they often fly under the radar. They prefer their humor planned and understated—a subtle laugh line thoughtfully woven into a speech or presentation versus a joke told on the fly. Sensitive and cheerful, Sweethearts stay away from teasing at the risk of hurting feelings (plus prefer not to be the subject of others' teasing), and instead use humor as a tool to lift up those around them and bring people together.

If you have an optimistic bent to your humor, aren't interested in the limelight, and prefer to plan out what you'll say (and how it will make people feel), you might lean toward the Sweetheart style.

The Magnet (Affiliative-Expressive)

Magnets have an ability to boost people's moods with unwavering good cheer. They keep things positive, warm, and uplifting, avoiding controversial or upsetting humor while radiating charisma. Their delivery tends to be animated and sometimes even slapstick—they readily slip into impersonations and characters. Magnets often crack up when delivering a goofy joke because it's just too fun to tell—and are equally generous with their laughter when someone else takes the stage. If you do improv comedy (or have been told you should), have a reputation for giving great toasts at weddings (equally heart-felt and hilarious), and come home from parties with your cheeks sore from smiling, you might lean toward the Magnet style.

The Sniper (Aggressive-Subtle)

Snipers are edgy, sarcastic, and nuanced, unafraid to cross lines in pursuit of a laugh. They describe their humor as an "acquired taste"—one that not everyone will acquire—with a delivery that tends to be dry and under their breath. In group situations, they prefer to watch from the sidelines before making their move, giving them time to silently craft their next zinger. Don't expect them to laugh easily; in general, you need to earn the Sniper's laughter, which makes it even sweeter when you get it.

If you have a way of landing a deadly one-liner with a perfectly deadpan delivery, and aren't afraid to cross lines and go over people's heads, you might lean toward the Sniper style.

ADAPTING YOUR HUMOR STYLE

Most of us have some sense of which humor style comes most naturally, but these labels are by no means absolute. Our style can vary depending on our mood, the situation, and the audience. Some of us might love being the center of attention and telling loud, offensive jokes when out with a few close friends but are more likely to share a small, ironic observation in a crowd. Or we might be biting and sarcastic (in a loving way) at home with our partner but keep our humor light and positive with our team at work.

In fact, you not only *can* shift styles, but you *should*. As many comedians have shared with us, part of using humor effectively is being able to adjust your set and delivery depending on your read of the room. For instance, Stand-ups and Snipers tease to express affection but sometimes fail to realize that when taken too far, their humor can feel alienating to Magnets and Sweethearts. To keep the crowd on their side, it's important for Stand-ups and Snipers to know when to take their foot off the gas. On the flip side, Magnets and Sweethearts put themselves down to lift up others, but too much self-deprecation can undermine their power in the eyes of Stand-ups and Snipers.

Our humor style isn't hard-wired. There's power in not just gaining awareness of our own style—our preferences and tendencies in what we find funny and how we deliver our humor—but in recognizing when it might benefit us to shift. In the chapters that follow, we'll share stories from people who span the spectrum of styles. By the end, we hope you'll have a broader perspective on how to adapt your own sense of humor based on the context, in a way that's authentic to you.

Remember, the bar for humor in the business world is extremely low. The goal isn't to elicit raucous, rolling-on-the-floor laughter; it's simply to create a moment of connection. Often, all it takes is a mindset of levity to transform a relationship or moment.

"Sounds easy enough," you say. "We're in! Wait—what the hell is *'a mindset of levity?'"*

LEVITY, HUMOR, AND COMEDY

The health psychologist and author Kelly McGonigal draws an important distinction between the concepts of *movement* and *exercise*. Movement, she says, is anytime you use your body to engage with life. Exercise is simply the choice to move for a purpose.

We use this simple but important distinction with our students and clients to explain a concept that's foundational to what we

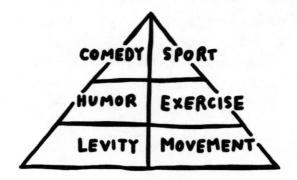

teach: the difference between *levity* and *humor*—and to go one step further, *comedy*.

Levity is a mindset—an inherent state of receptiveness to (and active seeking of) joy. Both levity and movement relate to how we navigate the world: naturally, and often without thinking. Both permeate everything we do, and even minor adjustments—something as simple as walking with your shoulders back instead of slouched, or buying an apple from an airport bodega with a smile instead of a scowl—have a major impact on how we feel and how people interact with us.

While levity is an inherent, baseline capability, *humor* is more intentional. Humor channels levity—just as exercise channels movement—toward a specific goal. We all have natural preferences in each realm: You might prefer yoga, soccer, or cycling, just as your sense of humor is drawn to certain styles of jokes, impersonations, or physical gags. Humor, like exercise, is something you can hone— something that requires skill and effort. It feels good,* and we know it's good for us, but sometimes it takes work.

Comedy is the practice of humor as a structured discipline. Like sport, comedy requires a dexterous command of technique and a great deal of training. Stand-up, improv, and sketch each require their own set of specialized skills, just as basketball, soccer, and hockey require different types of athletic ability. Only a select few compete at the professional level; not everyone wants to be on this level, and not everyone can. In this book, our goal isn't to turn you into a professional; we won't teach you to perform improv like Amy Poehler or tell jokes like Stephen Colbert—though we will study a few of their techniques the same way amateur athletes watch and

---

* With good reason: Laughter releases many of the same neurochemicals as a good workout, resulting in a feeling akin to a "runner's high." Beyond feeling similarly pleasurable, both also prime us for greater personal connection and resilience to stress. So in a way, Jillian Michaels and Amy Schumer have the same job.

learn from the pros. More important though, we'll teach you to navigate the world with more levity, and hopefully get you to hone and
flex your unique flavor of humor.

McGonigal says that "people often panic when they hear the
word 'exercise.'" Similarly, our students walk into class with trepidation, worried that we expect them to be fall-down funny. In fact,
we simply want to encourage them to embrace and revel in their
natural human tendency to levity, in the same way McGonigal
wants people to experience the inherent joy of movement.

If we hope to achieve one thing with this book, it's to engender
a greater sense of levity in your day-to-day life. While we'd love for
you to be a team captain in the next All-Star game, we care more
about getting you off the couch and dancing when a good song plays
on shuffle.

MEANWHILE, BACK AT THE FARM

By now, you're more or less caught up with the students in our class
at the Stanford Graduate School of Business.* They've completed
their humor audits (just as you will—read on!), and now they're
ready to start paying attention to the nuances of humor in their
lives—where they see it in the world, what they find funny, who
brings it out in them, and how they most naturally express it.

Over the course of the semester, our students experience a profound shift. What begins as a sobering, often (very) unfunny first
class (remember: "On Tuesday, I did not laugh once. Not once. Who
knew a class about humor could be so depressing?") ends with students reporting significantly more joy and more laughter in their
lives.

This shift is about more than their becoming funnier: They become more generous with their laughter. They notice opportunities

---

*Which means you have an honorary degree of some type. Congratulations!

for humor that would otherwise pass them by. The mindset of look-ing for reasons to be delighted becomes a habit.

In a very real way, they learned how to move a little more fluidly, how to exercise with better form, and play their favorite (amateur) sport with better results—just as you will. When you walk around on the precipice of a smile, you'll be surprised how many things you encounter that push you over the edge. So, repeat after us:

"I promise to laugh more. Even on Tuesday."

THE HUMOR AUDIT*
WHAT DOES HUMOR LOOK LIKE IN MY LIFE?

This exercise is intended to spark self-awareness about various aspects of your unique sense of humor, so you can more easily tap into it on a moment's notice. Remember, this is about activating a mindset of levity, not achieving viral hilarity. So when you reflect on moments of humor, think also about moments that created delight, joy, amusement, or even just a smile.

1. When was the last time you really laughed?
2. In general, who or what makes you laugh the most in your life?
3. When was the last time you made someone else laugh?
4. Who do *you* feel the funniest around; who appreciates your humor?

Pro Tip: If you find yourself struggling with this mission, get an outside perspective. Ask friends, family members, and colleagues to answer the questions with (and about) you.

Reflection: What surprised you? Were certain questions easier or more difficult? What realizations or questions did this spark?

---

*Feel free to share with your accountant, not because it's a real audit but because accountants need to laugh, too.

CHAPTER 2

Your Brain

on Humor

"Humor is by far the most significant activity of the human brain."

—*Edward de Bono*

Let's talk cocktails. But not the delicious, tequila-based kind.

When we laugh, our brains release a cocktail of hormones that make us feel happier (dopamine), more trusting (oxytocin), less stressed (lowered cortisol), and even slightly euphoric (endorphins). By working humor into our professional interactions, we can serve our colleagues this powerful hormone cocktail, and in doing so we can literally change their—and our—brain chemistry on the spot.

LAUGHTER,
A BRAIN COCKTAIL

EUPH ORIC
LESS STRESSED
TRUSTING
HAPPY

But the neuroscience is only one part of the story. There's also a wealth of behavioral research linking the use of humor in business to increase:

- **Power,** by enhancing others' perceptions of our status and intelligence, influencing their behavior and decision making, and making our ideas more memorable.
- **Bonds,** by quickening the path to trust and self-disclosure in new relationships, and making us feel more satisfied with our relationships over time.

- **Creativity**, by helping us see connections we previously missed, and making us feel psychologically safe enough to share our risky or unconventional ideas.
- **Resilience**, by reducing stress in the moment, allowing us to bounce back more quickly from setbacks.

Mark Twain is said to have observed, "The human race has only one really effective weapon, and that is laughter." By understanding exactly how this secret weapon alters our brain chemistry, psychology, and behavior, we can become more adept at wielding it strategically.

So let's dive into the science of these four benefits laughter can bring in the workplace: power, bonds, creativity, and resilience.

Power

CLIMBING THE LADDER OF LEVITY

The first time Naomi used humor in a high-stakes professional setting was an accident. It started (like all good stories) in a conference room.

She was early in her career, working in The Deloitte Greenhouse, a special forces team of strategy consultants that designed and facilitated workshops for groups of Deloitte's highest priority clients. She'd been asked to facilitate a team dynamics session for an executive team, most of whom were fifteen to twenty years her senior. A young(ish) Naomi was floating solo on a makeshift raft in a sea of houndstooth blazers.

One of those houndstooth blazers, a man named Craig, had been posturing all session, outwardly disengaged and skeptical. His fingers were laced behind his head, shoulders relaxed, chair leaned back so far it was straining both credulity and the Steelcase springs holding it together. This man was the chest-beating alpha of the group, clearly signaling to any person—or primate, for that matter—who held the highest status in the conference room that day.

Naomi was in the middle of explaining how to tailor your communication to different personality styles, when Craig interrupted: "Can you cut to the part where you just teach me how to make my team do what I want?"

The room stiffened. Somewhere, a record screeched.

All heads slowly swiveled from Craig to Naomi.

Without thinking, she playfully shot back: "Great question, Craig. You're thinking of the workshop I run on mind control. That one's next week, and you're welcome to join."

A long second passed while Naomi wondered if she'd just torched her career. But then, the room erupted in laughter and all eyes turned back to Craig.

His comment had been piercing, challenging, borderline disrespectful. From the dynamics of the room, it was clear that Craig was not accustomed to being challenged—particularly by someone so far his junior. And yet, for the first time all day, he was smiling.

"I respect you," he said, rocking back in his chair. "You can continue."

"Thank you," Naomi replied. "I was planning on it."

Almost immediately, the energy shifted. For the rest of the workshop, Craig was engaged and respectful, and his executive team followed suit. The room relaxed and people began participating more freely and casually with materially better ideas. Naomi relaxed as well, and as a result, so did her delivery of the content. What's more, Naomi began to feel more like herself, shifting from a place of fear to one of presence, engagement, and flow.

After the session, Craig and Naomi exchanged a few words about her career, and he seemed in good spirits. She would later learn that Craig sent a note to her CEO lauding the workshop, and Naomi personally, for her insights and command of the room— a gesture that set in motion a chain of events that would open new doors for her career.

In large part thanks to a silly little joke about mind control.

. . . Or *was* it the mind control?

GAINING STATUS

A key concept regarding humor is its relationship to status.

In one study, some of our colleagues from the Second City retreat—Brad Bitterly, Maurice Schweitzer, and Alison Wood Brooks—recruited participants to write and present testimonials for VisitSwitzerland, a fictional travel company. What the group didn't know is that the first two "participants" who read their testimonials were research assistants. Half of their prewritten testimonials were serious, the other half were funny (e.g., serious testimonial "The mountains are great for skiing and hiking. It's amazing!" vs. humorous testimonial "The mountains are great for skiing and hiking, and the flag is a big plus!"). . . . *

When participants were asked to rate the presenters on a handful of qualities, those presenting the humorous testimonial were perceived as 5 percent more competent, 11 percent more confident, and 37 percent higher in status.

In other words, a six-word throwaway pun at the end of a testimonial meaningfully swung opinions.

Humor impacts not just our perceptions of others, but also how we treat them. In this same study, when participants were asked to choose a group leader for a subsequent task, the research assistant

---

*While this barely seems like a joke, you must understand that research studies are vast deserts of dry technical language, where even a tiny drop of levity is a welcome oasis. Not unlike corporate America.

with the funny testimonial was significantly more likely to be chosen, simply based on this (not particularly good) joke.

Similarly, in the conference room with Craig that day, Naomi used a dash of humor to signal bravery, confidence, and mental agility, augmenting her perceived status and power.

LOOKING SMART

Having a sense of humor—both the ability to generate humor and to appreciate it—has repeatedly been found to correlate with measures of intelligence.

In one truly inspired study, researchers Daniel Howrigan and Kevin MacDonald had participants craft humorous replies to ridiculous questions ("If you could experience what it's like to be a different kind of animal for a day, what kind of animal would you *not* want to be, and why?") as well as draw the "funniest, most amusing-looking depiction of each animal that you can."

A set of anonymous judges then rated the participants' pictures and stories on their humor. Participants whose submissions were rated funniest had scored the highest on earlier general intelligence tests.[*]

Unlike thick-rimmed glasses, reading your comic books behind a big dictionary, or pretending you don't own a television set, humor is a sign of intelligence that can't be faked. Or in the words of Tina Fey, "You can always tell how smart someone is by what they laugh at."

GETTING (MORE OF) WHAT YOU WANT

Beyond gaining status and looking smart, humor is a powerful tool for influence in one of the last places we may think to use it: around the negotiation table.

In one experiment, researchers Karen O'Quin and Joel Aronoff asked participants to negotiate with an "art dealer" (research assistant) over the purchase price of a piece of art. Half of the research assistants made a final offer that was significantly above the participants' last bid, stating simply "My final offer is X." The other half offered the same amount, but said with a smile, "My final offer is X . . . and I'll throw in my pet frog."

Here's the kicker: For the final offers accompanied by the pet frog line, buyers were willing to pay, on average, an *18 percent higher price*. What's more, the buyers later reported enjoying the task more and feeling less tension with the seller.

Think about that—the participants paid more, and they walked away feeling better about both the negotiation and their relationship with the seller than those who paid less. All thanks to a smile and a lighthearted comment.

In another negotiation study by researchers Terri Kurtzberg,

---

[*]A bit more granularity for our data geeks: Researchers found a significant positive correlation between measured general intelligence and humor ratings, where an increase in humor ratings of .29 standard deviations on average predicted an increase in intelligence scores of 1 standard deviation. Aren't statistics fun?

Charles Naquin, and Liuba Belkin, participants were paired up and assigned the role of recruiter or job candidate. In the simulation, they would be negotiating via email over an employment compensation package, each element of which (e.g., salary, bonus, insurance coverage, vacation time) had an associated point value. The goal was to walk away from the table with more points. In the humor condition, one person from each pair of participants (either the recruiter or candidate) shared a *Dilbert* comic strip about negotiations before the simulation began.

Not only did the comic-strip-sharing individuals enjoy a 33 percent higher point value than their negotiating counterparts, but the pairs in the humor condition reported 31 percent higher trust in each other and reported feeling 16 percent greater satisfaction with how the negotiation went overall.

Humor charms and disarms. Even small gestures of levity are powerful in negotiations, in part because they spark human connection—and when we connect as people, we often get more of what we both want.

STANDING OUT AND BEING REMEMBERED

Humor also helps us remember. By flooding our reward center with the neurotransmitter dopamine, humor engenders deeper levels of focus and long-term retention. In other words, using humor makes your content more engaging in the moment *and* more memorable after the fact.

This finding was illustrated in a Pew Research poll, showing that viewers of humorous news shows like *The Daily Show* and *The Colbert Report* remembered more about current events than people who consumed information from newspapers, cable news, or network news. And in one study, researchers found that people who watched a humorous film clip before taking a brief short-term memory test recalled *more than twice as much information* as people who took the same test after simply sitting doing nothing for the same duration.

It works in the classroom, too: Another study by researcher Avner Ziv published in the *Journal of Experimental Education* showed that students who were taught class material with humor retained more of the class learnings, scoring 11 percent higher on their final exams.

That's why it's not uncommon for politicians to include professional comedians among their cadre of speechwriters. During his 2011 State of the Union address, President Obama commented on the need to increase government efficiency with the following example: "The Interior Department is in charge of salmon while they're in freshwater. But the Commerce Department handles them when they're in saltwater." He paused. "I hear it gets even more complicated once they're smoked." The room erupted in laughter.*

When NPR surveyed its listeners, asking which three words most stood out from the SOTU address, can you guess the word most frequently mentioned?

---

* No matter your politics, you have to admit Obama has major "dad-joke" energy.

As the comedian John Sherman says, "If people are laughing, it means they're paying attention."

Bonds

BUILDING BRIDGES

The Obama White House wasn't the only administration that knew how to have a little fun at work. Keith Hennessey, a leading economic adviser to President George W. Bush, told us that W's staff was consistently brought closer together through gags, pranks, and a whole lot of levity.

A few years earlier, in 2005, it was future Federal Reserve chair Ben Bernanke's first day on the job as chairman of President Bush's Council of Economic Advisers. Bernanke had come to the Oval Office to deliver his first major presentation to the president, Hennessey, and more than a dozen other senior White House officials, including Vice President Dick Cheney, Senior Adviser Karl Rove, Director of Legislative Affairs Candi Wolff, and National Economic Council director Al Hubbard. Needless to say, the stakes were high.

The president and his advisers took their seats, arranged in a large circle around the edges of the Oval, and as Bernanke started speaking, the president interrupted him—with a lighthearted joshing for coupling his dark gray suit with *tan socks* (cue sirens of the fashion police).

Everyone in the room chuckled. Bernanke, newer to the group and more reserved, was momentarily flustered but quickly regained his composure and got through the rest of the briefing. After the meeting, though, Hennessey and Hubbard recognized that Bush's gentle ribbing had presented an opportunity to show solidarity with their new colleague.

So they concocted a plan.

When it was time for Bernanke's second major briefing to the president, the senior advisers shuffled into the Oval Office. As they took their seats, they each ensured they were positioned just right—to reveal their matching tan socks.

A wide grin spread across President Bush's face as the room erupted in laughter, the president's chops effectively busted. He turned to his veep: "Dick, can you believe what they—" and realized he, too, was in on the joke. The president threw up his hands to another wave of laughter. Then Bernanke and his team began the meeting, a bit more cheerfully than before.

"Policy Time" meeting in the Oval Office, held on 21 July 2005. President Bush is surrounded by his tan-socked VP and team of senior advisors.

"It was a trivial thing," Hennessey later recalled, "but it was a wonderful bonding moment. The president, the vice president, and all the advisers together, sharing this little moment of joviality."

During our conversations, Hennessey detailed a long list of gags and pranks like these—saran-wrapping Karl Rove's car in the parking lot, explaining an important economic policy decision using sock puppets. In the highest office of the country, tackling some of the most substantive issues at hand, Hennessey explained, levity created a sense of trust and cohesion that "made it easier for us to function as a team, to work together, for the president and on behalf of the country."

ACCELERATING THE PATH TO TRUST

Maya Angelou said: "I don't trust anyone who doesn't laugh."

It's a keen observation—and one backed by science.

Back to our humor hormone cocktail: Laughter triggers the release of oxytocin, often referred to as the "trust hormone" because of the way it prompts our brain to create emotional bonds. No wonder oxytocin is released during sex and childbirth—both moments when, evolutionarily speaking, we benefit from feelings of closeness and trust with the other person involved, even if that relationship is brand new.

In one study, researchers Alan Gray, Brian Parkinson, and Robin Dunbar had pairs of strangers sit together for five minutes and watch a movie clip. Half watched a blooper reel from a popular TV comedy—one that had been pretested to get lots of laughs. The rest watched an emotionally neutral clip—think a nature channel documentary, or the lesser-known "Fifty Shades of Grayscale."*

When researchers asked participants to write a message to the person they had just met, the pairs who had watched the blooper clip disclosed significantly more personal information. And when a panel of observers watched these pairs converse, they rated the interactions between the blooper clip pairs as 30 percent more intimate than the ones between the pairs who had watched the neutral clip.

---

*Just a slideshow of gray wallpapers. Maybe not as popular as its namesake, but pretty useful if you're redecorating.

In short: Shared laughter quickens the path to candor and vulnerability. What's more, it's one of the few ways to release oxytocin at work that's still permitted by HR.

WAYS TO INCREASE "TRUST HORMONE" OXYTOCIN AT WORK

Rx	notes
SEX	technically not allowed
CHILDBIRTH	not encouraged medically
LAUGHTER	no known HR violations

MAKING RELATIONSHIPS LAST

Shared laughter doesn't just create closeness in the moment. It's equally effective at strengthening relationships over time. While the tan socks gag lasted less than a minute, Hennessey says the sense of camaraderie and cohesion it created "lasted well beyond the meeting."

This trend has been demonstrated in the lab. In one study, the psychologist Doris Bazzini and colleagues recruited fifty-two couples and gave each individual a relationship satisfaction questionnaire. The couples were then assigned to one of four groups.

In the first group, couples were asked to tell stories about moments of "Shared Laughter" that had occurred within the last three months—what happened in these moments, what led to them, and what happened afterward. In the other three groups, couples were asked to tell stories about moments of "Independent Laughter" (moments when they each laughed with someone else), "Shared Positivity" (moments they shared that made them feel good about their relationship with each other), and "Independent Positivity" (moments that made them feel good about their relationship with someone else).

At the end of the study, the couples who were asked to reminisce about moments of shared laughter reported being 23 percent more satisfied in their relationships than the couples in the other three groups.*

While you may not be romantically involved with your co-workers, there are compelling parallels between our romantic and work relationships. Just consider for a moment how much time you spent with your partner last week versus your closest colleague (your "work wife/husband").†

Creativity
SPARKING IDEAS AND FUELING INNOVATION

Fostering an environment where employees produce their most artful work is an art in itself. During his tenure as head of Apple's Creative Design Studio, Hiroki Asai used humor as a critical catalyst for creative thinking.

"Fear is the greatest killer of creativity," Asai explained, "and

---

*Think of how much money you would pay for a therapist to achieve that type of result. This book just pays for itself.

†The 2019 Bureau of Labor Statistics' American Time Use Survey reported that the average person spends thirteen years and two months at work. In contrast, people spend an average of only 328 days socializing with friends over the course of a lifetime. Thus the classic adage: "Keep your friends close, and your middle managers closer."

humor is the most effective tool I've found for insulating cultures from fear."

For Asai, there was no better place to deploy humor than the All Hands meeting, where all two-thousand-plus creatives in his charge gathered together in one place. These meetings were deadly serious—and very funny. Months before each, he would assemble a team tasked with carefully planning an experience designed to get an auditorium full of employees laughing together. Once, they shot a video of employees dressed up as the Blue Man Group. During another, they showed a series of gag videos shot to look like chase scenes in hot pursuit of a man (Hiroki) on the run. And at another, a flash mob gospel choir emerged from the audience. The common denominator across all of them was their unexpectedness and ability to make everyone laugh.

When convening your entire organization, every moment counts, which is exactly why Hiroki invested so much in bringing people together in unusual ways. Across the organization, he saw firsthand how fear corroded inclusive creative processes, and how levity and humor unlocked them. Humor, he says, "chased fear from the system," allowing people to think more freely, speak more openly, and entertain new scenarios and approaches.

GOOD IDEAS CAN COME FROM (ALMOST) ANYWHERE

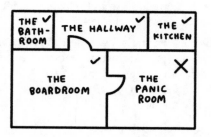

ENHANCING MENTAL AGILITY

To understand the connection between laughter and creativity, meet Duncker's Candle Problem, a cognitive test created by psychologist Alice Isen and her colleagues.

It's a real-life challenge in which participants are given a candle, a box of tacks, and matches:

Yes, that's a candle.

Individuals in the study are told that their mission is to attach the candle to the wall, using only the items on the table, in such a way that wax doesn't drip onto the table below when the candle is lit.

The correct solution is to empty the tacks from the box and use them to tack the box to the wall, creating a shelf to hold the candle. That might seem simple enough, but arriving at this solution requires your brain to overcome what's called functional fixedness—a cognitive bias that makes it hard for people to see how to use an object in any way other than the one in which it is traditionally used (in this case, seeing that box as anything other than a receptacle for the tacks).

Five-year-old children show no signs of functional fixedness because they haven't yet learned the traditional rules that govern the adult world—for example, that the wall is a wall and not a canvas for crayon art; that the dog is a pet, not a small horse to ride on; and that peas are for eating and not putting up noses. But by the time we reach adulthood, we have a hard time seeing any possibilities beyond the explicit intended purpose of an object.

Like this tack box as a shelf for the, ahem, candle.

To see how humor factored into participants' ability to solve this puzzle, Isen and her colleagues had half of them watch an emotionally neutral video before taking on the challenge, while the other half watched a humorous one.*

The results were striking: More than *twice* as many people who watched the funny video solved the puzzle. It's not that laughter made the second group smarter; it's that laughter helped them overcome their functional fixedness and see new connections and associations (in many ways, the crux of all creative processes).

On the surface, the candle challenge may seem trivial. But as author Dan Pink explains, this kind of mental flexibility is critical—particularly in a rapidly transforming global economy in which more routine, rules-based work is easier than ever to outsource or automate, given that low-cost providers can do it cheaper and AI can do it faster (and better, and cheaper, and with more interesting premises for sci-fi movies starring Sigourney Weaver).

---

*There's a reason *America's Emotionally Neutralest Home Videos* never made it past the first season.

In today's workplace, right-brained creativity and lateral think-ing are at a premium. We are constantly tackling our own versions of the candle challenge, and the winners will likely be those with some crayon art on the walls.

THINKING OUTSIDE THE BOX

Attempts at humor ignite the creativity center of our brains with an intensity unmatched by simple brainstorming. In an experiment run by Ori Amir and Irving Biederman from the University of Southern California, professional comedians from the Groundlings Theatre in Los Angeles, amateur comedians, and ordinary civilians were asked to come up with a clever caption for a *New Yorker* draw-ing. Half of the participants brainstormed humorous captions, the other half nonhumorous captions. During the exercise, both groups underwent MRI scanning to determine how the physiology of their brains responded to the task.

Spoiler alert: The comedians' captions were better. But across the board, the results showed that when participants were in the process of brainstorming humorous captions, they experienced heightened activity in the brain region associated with creativity, as well as in other regions associated with higher-level functions like learning and recognition (the temporal association regions and the medial prefrontal cortex).

What's more, evidence suggests that this creativity boost persists long after the initial task. In a set of studies led by Barry Kudrowitz at Massachusetts Institute of Technology, comedians, professional product designers, and students were asked to create cartoon cap-tions followed by a brainstorming test. The results revealed not only that comedians generated 20 percent more ideas during the brain-storming test than other groups, but also that the ideas they gener-ated were rated as 25 percent more creative by others.

In words attributed to Albert Einstein, "Creativity is intelligence having fun." Let your intelligence live a little.

FOSTERING PSYCHOLOGICAL SAFETY

The relationship between safety and work performance is robust. As researcher Amy Edmondson and her colleagues have found, psychological safety—the belief that we won't be punished or ridiculed when we make a mistake—makes us more open-minded, resilient, motivated, and persistent. When we feel safe enough to make light of our mistakes, in other words, it gives us the courage to take on bigger and bolder risks.

As Hiroki saw it: "Ultimately, a culture of levity creates a safe place for employees. When you feel safe and feel like you're being led through levity versus fear, you're much more apt to take chances. You're more likely to try things without worrying about being ridiculed, or ostracized. You're more willing to innovate—to push new ideas and to push against old ideas."

The link between humor and psychological safety lies in laughter: Even the *anticipation* of laughing has been shown to decrease cortisol (our "stress hormone") and epinephrine (our "fight or

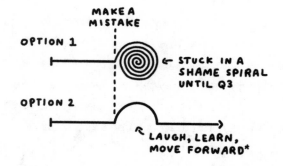

HUMOR HELPS US
MOVE FORWARD

MAKE A MISTAKE

OPTION 1 — STUCK IN A SHAME SPIRAL UNTIL Q3

OPTION 2 — LAUGH, LEARN, MOVE FORWARD*

* LET'S ASSUME NO ONE BROKE THE LAW

flight" hormone) by 39 percent and 70 percent respectively, making us feel safer, calmer, and less stressed.

And when we're less stressed, we do better work. In 2007, researchers with the Baltimore Memory Study measured participants' salivary cortisol levels and then tested their cognitive functioning on seven key metrics: language, processing speed, eye-hand coordination, executive functioning, verbal memory and learning, visual memory, and visuoconstruction. Remarkably, researchers found a correlation between lower cortisol (i.e., stress) levels and better performance in six of the seven tests (Visuoconstruction had no effect and is unimpressed by how chill and unstressed you are.).

In short: Laughter decreases cortisol, and lower cortisol means better performance. Unless perhaps you are a visuoconstruction worker.

Resilience

SURVIVING AND THRIVING

In September 2001, Mike Nemeth was a sophomore in the United States Military Academy at West Point. When two hijacked airliners crashed into the World Trade Center fifty miles south in Manhattan, he and his classmates watched the devastating aftermath unfold, knowing that their lives, like the lives of so many, would never be the same. War—in which they would almost certainly be called on to fight—felt imminent. Amid the gravity of the moment, Nemeth vowed to do anything he could to lift the collective spirits of his fellow cadets.

He created an underground humor factory within the barracks, publishing a satirical newspaper with headlines like ARMY: BIN LADEN AND AL QAEDA TO BLAME FOR FOOTBALL LOSS and CADET CASUAL TAKES THE WORLD BY STORM that poked fun at the shared—and sometimes painful—experiences of academy life and the looming international conflict.

Knowing that the officers might shut down his unorthodox operation if discovered, he distributed the paper covertly, sliding it into plastic page protectors taped to the inside of latrine stall doors. And that's how his newspaper found its audience and its name: *Center Stall*.

News of the paper spread quickly among the cadets as muffled laughter echoed from the stalls. Nemeth's classmates clandestinely passed him content ideas; bathroom trips to check for new installments became a daily occurrence.

It didn't take long for the Army brass to find out. Technically, Nemeth was breaking the rules. But they also saw the impact his publications had on the cadets—how it shifted the mood in small but meaningful ways. And so the officers turned a blind eye. And over time, officers and cadets alike would embrace *Center Stall* as an integral part of the tightly woven fabric of West Point culture.

In a time of extreme uncertainty, mourning, and stress, this sliver of levity helped the cadets cope with a harrowing new reality. As the abolitionist clergyman Henry Ward Beecher noted: "A person without a sense of humor is like a wagon without springs. It's jolted by every pebble on the road." We all need a buffer against life's shake-ups, big or small, and humor is one of the best we've got.

COPING WITH STRESS

It's harder than ever to stay healthy at work. As recent work by Joel Goh, Jeff Pfeffer, and Stefanos Zenios reveals, workplace stress—fueled by long hours, job insecurity, and work-life imbalance—contributes to at least 120,000 deaths each year and accounts for up to $190 billion in healthcare costs.

In other words, work is killing us.

Luckily, humor is a powerful insulator. By now, we all know that laughter suppresses cortisol, our body's security alarm system, which is also linked to anxiety and increased risk of depression. By keeping cortisol levels in check, humor bolsters our emotional resilience in difficult times.

Humor doesn't just help reduce stress, though—it also helps people cope in times of acute *distress* as well.

In one study, researchers Dacher Keltner and George Bonanno looked at the effects of laughter on the bereavement process. They recruited forty people who had lost a loved one in the previous six months and asked them to describe their relationship with the deceased.

When researchers reviewed the taped interviews, they found that the participants who displayed genuine laughter (known as "Duchenne" laughter) when talking about their loved one had reported 80 percent less anger and 35 percent less distress on a subsequent questionnaire than those feigning laughter or not laughing at all. The genuine laughers also reported feeling significantly more positive emotions and indicated increased satisfaction with their current social relationships.

While these findings are of course correlational, emerging work aims to better understand causation. In one study, researchers Shelley Crawford and Nerina Caltabiano developed an eight-week program that taught specific skills relating to the use and enjoyment of humor in everyday life. Each week, a different skill was taught in a one-hour learning module presented by an instructor to a small group. After the eight weeks, those in the humor skills group reported fewer instances of depression, lower stress, a higher proportion of positive to negative feelings, and even significantly increased perceptions of control.

(AH—AH—AH—AH) STAYING ALIVE

Laughter is the best medicine. (Actually, medicine is the best medicine. But laughter just might help you avoid needing quite so much of it.)

THE BEST MEDICINE

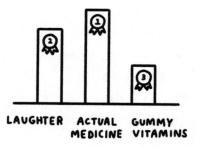

LAUGHTER   ACTUAL   GUMMY
MEDICINE   VITAMINS

Physiologically, laughter confers meaningful benefits, increasing blood flow and muscle relaxation and reducing the arterial wall stiffness associated with cardiovascular disease.

In one truly Patch Adams–inspired study by researchers Martin Brutsche and team, patients with chronic obstructive pulmonary disease experienced improved lung function after being entertained by a clown.

This is totally true, and totally weird, so we're just going to leave this one alone and hope you're still able to sleep tonight.

Still not convinced?

Then how would you like to live *forever*?

Okay, not forever. But research *does* reveal a correlation between sense of humor and longevity. In a fifteen-year longitudinal study of more than fifty thousand people, Norwegian researchers from the Norwegian University of Science and Technology found that both women and men with a strong sense of humor lived longer—even in spite of illness and infection.* Specifically, women who scored high on the use of humor had a 48 percent lower risk of death from all causes, a 73 percent lower risk of death from heart disease, and an 83 percent lower risk of death from infection; men who scored high

---

*And this is in the subzero temperatures of Norway. Imagine what it could do in Palm Springs!

on humor, meanwhile, had a 74 percent lower risk of death from infection.

*   *   *

So there you have it. Humor can be power-enhancing for us and intoxicating to others. It fosters meaningful connections, unlocks creativity, makes tense situations less stressful, and helps us survive and thrive through life's ups and downs.

CHAPTER 3

The Anatomy

of Funny

"Comedy is simply a funny way of being serious."

—*Peter Ustinov*

It's a typical Tuesday morning in June, and Seth Meyers strolls into his office in 30 Rockefeller Plaza. His nightly talk show, *Late Night with Seth Meyers*, is filmed right down the hall from Studio 8G, where he previously worked as head writer for *Saturday Night Live* and earned his reputation as one of the sharpest (and downright nicest) people in comedy.

Among his morning's work, Seth reviews a long list of jokes for the show's opening monologue. The monologue will ultimately feature just a dozen jokes—delivered in rapid succession—about the day's news. In the few hours since last night's show wrapped, his heroic writing team of sixteen caffeine-addled geniuses has scoured the headlines, pinpointed dozens of stories, and deftly fashioned them into more than one hundred jokes, from which they'll choose the twelve that will ultimately air.*

That's *one hundred jokes,* turned around in just eight hours (including naps), to produce material for *seven minutes* of his hour long show. By the afternoon, Seth's writing team will whittle the list down to eighty. Out of those, twenty-five will make it to the dress rehearsal. And finally, the lucky dozen.

This is staggering—and it's the norm! In writers' rooms across New York and LA, similar magic is in motion. From *Last Week Tonight with John Oliver* to *The Tonight Show with Jimmy Fallon* to *The Late Show with Stephen Colbert,* small armies of writers are cranking out

---

*Which also means that eighty-eight get left on the cutting room floor. What a waste! Surely there must be a way to recycle the unused jokes, donating them to dads or tax accountants.

thousands of jokes competing to be good enough for prime-time television.

If you're anything like us, you've watched many of these shows (and others with different formats, like *SNL*) for years, awestruck at how they manage to produce a steady stream of content that is funny, timely, and artfully crafted to tackle some of the most sensitive and socially charged issues of the moment. Perhaps you've wondered: How in the world do they do it?

The mastery of these extraordinary writers is a combination of raw comedic athleticism and years of hard work: performing in dimly lit improv theaters, sharpening their material on unforgiving audiences at open mic nights, and writing sketch upon sketch that might never see the light of day.

As we've learned from Seth's team and the dozens of other comedians and writers we've studied and worked with over the last five years, comedy is an art, but it's also a well-honed craft—with common techniques that show up across comedians and formats.

In this chapter, we'll explore the most common and impactful techniques that dozens of comedian friends, teachers, performers, and writers have graciously shared with us throughout this journey. Not so you can quit your job to become the next Dave Chappelle, but to help you understand the basic principles of how humor works—so that you can better appreciate it, craft it, and bring more of it in your everyday life.

The Basics: Truth and Misdirection

A common misconception among our clients and students is that humor involves inventing something from thin air. In reality, humor more often comes simply from noticing the oddities and absurdities in the world around you and identifying them in an unexpected manner.

To better understand the underlying patterns and mechanics of humor, let's deconstruct a simple joke.

Imagine you're at a dinner party and a guest walks in thirty minutes after the first course, announcing apologetically:

"Sorry I'm late. I didn't want to come."

You might find this funny, or at least mildly amusing. Here's why:

PRINCIPLE #1: AT THE HEART OF HUMOR IS TRUTH

This statement is funny because it's truer and more direct than what we're used to hearing—typically some tenuous excuse designed to disguise the fact that we just came from binge-watching *The Great British Bake Off.*

Truth lies at the heart of all humor. It's why *Seinfeld*—the "show about nothing"—was so successful: The entire premise was navigating common social interactions that drive us nuts. The low talker, the close talker, shrinkage, guys who paint their faces for sporting events—the list goes on. Viewers laughed at these people and scenarios because of a shared recognition, unconsciously registering "I do that" or "I've seen people do that" or "He's right! Hockey fans *are* ridiculous."

IT'S FUNNY BECAUSE IT'S TRUE

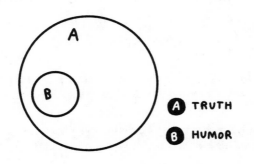

A TRUTH

B HUMOR

Shared truths create the foundation for humor. So instead of asking yourself what is funny, start by asking what is true. We'll find humor from there.

PRINCIPLE #2: ALL HUMOR CONTAINS SURPRISE AND MISDIRECTION

Laughter also springs from the unexpected, when we think someone will zig and instead they ham sandwich. Social scientists explain this principle via the Incongruity-Resolution Theory, which holds that humor comes from the incongruity between what we expect and what actually happens. This is a fancy way of saying that people like being surprised. When the setup of the joke leads our brain in one direction and the punch line unexpectedly pivots to the Backstreet Boys, we experience incongruity.

See what we did there?* Hearing the phrase "one direction" in the first part of the sentence, you likely expected that "another direction" would follow in the second . . . and you were surprised to discover a highly uncool reference to a boy band from the nineties.

At the recognition of an incongruity like this, your prefrontal cortex springs into action to resolve it, generating the experience of humor. And then you get the joke. They were *both* highly uncool references to boy bands.†

Your prefrontal cortex high-fives itself, eats a cookie, and goes back to sleep.

Plenty of humor falls flat not for lack of a clever idea, but for lack of misdirection. Either the expectation isn't adequately established or the punch line doesn't adequately defy it.

Later on, we'll offer some simple techniques for creating sur-

---

*For nonmillennials: One Direction was a wildly popular English-Irish pop boy band of the 2010s. We hope we don't have to tell you who the Backstreet Boys were.

†People say analyzing humor is like dissecting a frog: Few people are interested and the frog dies. This is where we hit our stride.

prise and misdirection. But first things first: Clearly some truths are riper for humor than others. With that, let's explore some strategies for finding those truths.

Part 1: Finding the Funny (Mine Your Life for Truth)

Seth Meyers's team finds humorous truths by immersing themselves in the news. Luckily, the rest of us don't need to limit our source material to depressing current events. We can mine our own lives for truth about ourselves and the people around us. That's why when comedian Sarah Cooper visited our class and ran a comedy skills workshop with our students, the first thing she had them do was make simple observations about their lives. "Never look for what's funny," she told our students, "Look for what's true and go from there."

This approach echoes that of Del Close, whom many consider to be the father of improvisational comedy. As the driving force behind improv culture in Chicago for more than thirty years, Close and his methods inspired comedy greats like Bill Murray, Tim Meadows, Horatio Sanz, Gilda Radner, and Chris Farley. He once said, "The freshest, most interesting comedy is not based on mother-in-law jokes or Jack Nicholson impressions,* but on exposing our own personalities." To find humor, Close believed, we must examine the qualities, opinions, predilections, and feelings that make us who we are.

In the world of *Seinfeld*, for example, George loves naps; Kramer loves Junior Mints; Elaine loves the Sponge; Jerry loves Superman, cereal, the Mets, and leaving his apartment door unlocked. The

---

* Unless you're Jack Nicholson, who does a killer Jack Nicholson impression.

humor lies in the small observations that highlight these simple truths.

But you don't have to rely only on your own observations, thoughts, and feelings; you can also create humor out of the assumptions that other people make about you. To get at some of these assumptions, comedian Alex Weber had our students play a game of personal Mad Libs. The students did this with their classmates, but you can ask just about anyone—at dinner parties, first dates, family holidays, the line at the DMV—to fill in the blank about you:

If I'm being honest, you seem like the kind of person who _____.*

Every one of us has quirks that are unique to our distinct personalities. And all of our lives are brimming with the seeds of humor—we just need some tools to discover them. Here are five simple techniques—which show up time and time again in the teachings of those who have spent their lives studying, performing, writing, and directing comedy—to get you started.

INCONGRUITY | NOTICE DIFFERENCES

When Sarah Cooper prompted our students to make simple observations about their lives, the first place she encouraged them to look was in areas of contrast, contradiction, and juxtaposition. This can mean noticing contrast within your own life—for example, you're a high-powered CEO at work but the eager personal assistant to your two teenage daughters at home, or your apartment is feng shui'd to the nines but your silverware drawer is Marie Kondo's personal hell.†

---

* This is how Jennifer learned that she seems like the kind of person who "would try to knock off a few emails while she is meditating" and how Naomi learned she seems like the kind of person who "brings s'mores supplies to every outdoor event 'just in case.'"

† Note: "Marie Kondo's personal hell" is only a figure of speech, not where she'll end up. Marie seems lovely and we imagine she is destined for a very tidy afterlife.

It can mean looking for differences between how you behave and how other people behave. For example, Sarah observed that she and her husband have very different packing styles when they travel:

It can also be personal incongruity over time, demonstrated by this bit from John Mulaney in which he observes how his appetite for risk has changed over the past two decades:

> *I smoked cocaine the night before my college graduation and now I'm afraid to get a flu shot.*

Sal Gentile, head writer for the *Closer Look* segment of *Late Night with Seth Meyers*, spends a lot of time focusing on the incongruity between how things in our political system are supposed to be and how they actually are. His segment explains and satirizes difficult political issues, often by using real clips from network news as the foundation of the humor. In today's news cycle more than ever, these incongruities aren't hard to find if you're looking for them. "And comedy," says Gentile, "is very good at framing these inconsistencies—at saying: 'Wait a minute, it's not supposed to be that way. Here's why that's weird.'"

And if none of those examples sparked ideas, try this angle on incongruity: If aliens suddenly landed on Earth, what would they find objectively illogical? Maybe the fact that the vending machine at your gym sells only Cheetos and cookies. Or this line from Jerry Seinfeld, highlighting the dynamic of owners picking up after their pets:

> *Dogs are the leaders of the planet. If you see two life forms, one of them's making a poop, the other one's carrying it for him, who would you assume is in charge?*

Incongruities, in a sense, are life's little misdirections. They are the world doing half—maybe all—the work for you in finding the funny.

EMOTION | NOTICE WHAT YOU FEEL

When Matt Klinman, former head writer for *The Onion* Video, gave our students advice on finding humorous content, he began by having each of them answer two simple questions: "What do you love?" and "What do you hate?"

Comedians pay close attention to emotion. What makes them feel embarrassed, happy, sad, proud, uncomfortable, or anything else—strongly? These outsized emotions can be stellar entry points for humor.

In addition to Matt's two questions, ask yourself: *What makes me happier than it objectively should? What frustrates me more than it seems to frustrate other people? What do I absolutely loathe, for no good reason?*

For example, maybe you feel exceptionally proud watching your four-year-old paint a decidedly unimpressive mermaid, irrationally happy opening a really fizzy can of seltzer, or inconsolably enraged by a flat one.

If you've ever been to a stand-up show (or watched an episode of *Curb Your Enthusiasm*), you know that many comedians rant about things that inspire irrational anger. Consider Kevin Hart's feelings about newly-in-love couples:

> *I don't mind seeing couples. I don't like seeing new couples. I can't stand new love. I hate it. That's me being honest. It's too much. . . . You ever see a couple that's newly in love try to share? You ever witness that? "Hey, babe. Hey. Babe. Hey, love button. Hey, love button. Hey, I got a little bit of juice left. You want some juice? Yeah? You wanna take a sip, I'll take a sip, you take a sip? You want to do it like that? You wanna go 'sip sip sip'" like that back and forth . . . I fuckin' hate it.*

Or Larry David, on Twitter, sharing his feelings about parties ("I hate parties. But *then* to have to go to an *after party? Are you kidding me?!?*"), college basketball ("Is there no vaccine for March Madness yet?!"), and birthday cards ("What do I do with old birthday cards? Keep them? Throw them away? They're useless. No more cards please. Email me.").

Making light of anger can be a tricky line to toe, but it's one you'll see comedians walk artfully.

When tapping into your anger in your own jokes, be sure to temper your temper. Directing a rant directly at a target will hurt feelings and won't feel funny. But if you're able to take those feelings and direct them at an amusing, fictionalized cartoon version of whatever it is that annoys you, other people may be able to feel how you feel without feeling personally attacked. And if you have the right touch, making fun of yourself and letting people know that your exaggerated reaction is partly *your* problem is a good way to set them at ease while still letting your feelings be known.

OPINION | NOTICE WHAT YOU THINK

David Iscoe, renowned sketch and improv comedy teacher at The Upright Citizens Brigade Theatre in New York, coaches his students to pay attention to the opinions they hold more strongly than others. This is less about your emotional quirks and more about your specific beliefs. Consider starting with norms or widely accepted behaviors that you think are appalling or absurd. Take, for example, how comedian Michelle Wolf thinks jogging is an objectively useless endeavor:

> *I run every day. I have no idea what I'm training for. 'Cause I am not physically gaining any skills. Like, the only way jogging is ever gonna help me in life is that at some point someone tries to rob me by chasing me for three to five miles at a moderately slow pace.*

Or how Sarah Cooper thinks we spend too much of our workday updating each other on our work rather than actually doing it:

WHAT ARE WE DOING AT WORK

Source: TheCooperReview.com

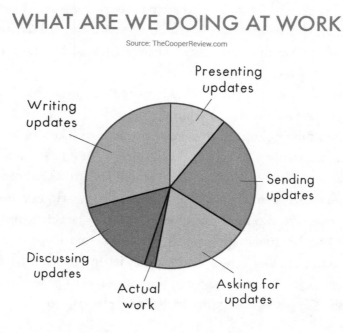

Presenting updates

Writing updates

Sending updates

Discussing updates

Actual work

Asking for updates

Think about things that make you say *I will never understand why
_____ is the norm.* You may be surprised by how many you come
up with. (And as you do, be chill and not judgy about it.)

PAIN | NOTICE WHAT HURTS OR MAKES YOU CRINGE

Think of your favorite stories to tell at a dinner party. Chances are
that some of them recount moments of misery or awkwardness
from your life. Arriving home after a date to discover you had a
chunk of asparagus stuck in your teeth. A "fun" family outing to
Disneyland punctuated by heat stroke, motion sickness, and a
three-hour line for a picture with Daisy Duck. Any trip to the
DMV.

Anne Libera, Director of Comedy Studies at The Second City,
cites pain as one of the three key ingredients for comedy (we'll
delve into the other two in chapter 7). We tend to laugh at stories
of another person's misfortune, not because human beings are
jerks—at least not all of them—but rather for the same reason
that we laugh at the punch line of a good joke. When a comedian
recounts a painful moment, our brains zero in on the incongruity
between the awfulness of the event and the blithe, cheery way it's
told.

After discussing how Los Angeles is an expensive city, comedian
Maronzio Vance recounts a phone call with his family after the fires
in Malibu in 2018:

> *They were like "Hey, we see Malibu is on fire. Are you all right?" And
> I was like . . . I'm flattered! That y'all think I live in Malibu. But
> I'm sorry to disappoint you but I live in Van Nuys where I am nice and
> poor and safe from the fires.*

And of course, plenty of pain becomes funny only after a certain amount of time has passed. The farther we get from the event

itself, the easier it is to gain some perspective and see the humor in it.

Like the old saying goes: Comedy equals tragedy plus time.

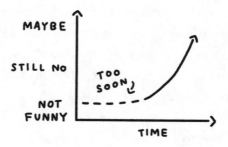

So the next time you find yourself in a miserable—or miserably awkward—situation, take solace in the fact that eventually it'll make for a great story. Eventually.

DELIGHT | NOTICE WHAT MAKES YOU SMILE

From a cognitive and behavioral perspective, there's more power than you might think in simply (a) being on the lookout for things that make you smile and (b) sharing them with others.

The former puts the *priming effect* to work—a principle in psychology wherein exposure to a stimulus impacts your response to a subsequent one. By reading this book, you've been primed for levity. And when we're primed for something, we are more likely to find it, faster and more often. This cycle is perpetuated with every new moment of delight. So, seek delight and ye shall find!

The latter harnesses laughter's high *emotional contagion*. Laughter is unique in that it mostly happens—and spreads—in the presence of others. So when you notice a dog in the park wearing a coat that looks exactly like one your best friend just bought, or when your kid opens her mouth and pretty much anything comes out—jot it down and share it. The way comedian James Breakwell did when he heard this:

> My six-year-old just called ranch dressing "salad frosting" and now
> I'll never call it anything else.

Breakwell didn't necessarily set out that morning to write a joke, but he did open himself up to the possibility of the world providing him with one.

As Mel Brooks said, "Life literally abounds in comedy if you just look around you."

Part 2: Forming the Funny

Many jokes follow the fundamental structure of **setup + punch line.** The setup is the observation or truth, and the punch line is what surprises audiences by flipping expectations (i.e., misdirection).

Sometimes, simple observations of life's truths and incongruities are enough for a laugh—but they don't always quite get there. In these times, a bit of massaging will help an idea cross the finish line to funny.

In those cases you can use one of these simple devices to help get you from setup to punch line:

EXAGGERATE

The first challenge that comedian Sarah Cooper gave our students once they'd made a long list of observations was to take each one and exaggerate it—playing with scale, magnitude, and hyperbole. This simple prompt had students delighted and shocked at how accessible humor could be with a bit of escalation.

When we heighten observations to the extreme, it creates misdirection by confounding the listener's expectations. Instead of the normal reaction people are expecting, you give them an outlandish one. On the next page, you can see how Cooper took her own simple observation—that airplane seats are ridiculously uncomfortable—to an extreme:

Sarah's done a few brilliant things here. She uses a familiar format, starts with the recognizable, and then exaggerates *to an extreme*. She also escalates her exaggeration as she moves down the seating chart—from the normal language you're used to seeing, like "First Class" and "Economy," to "Economy Discomfort," "Economy Agony," and beyond.

For a different flavor of exaggeration, consider this example from John Mulaney:

> *I got a massage recently. Went to a spa to get a massage. I went into the room to get the massage and the woman there told me to undress to my comfort level. So I put on a sweater and a pair of corduroy pants, and I felt safe.*

The observation behind this joke is clear: Mulaney is uncomfortable getting undressed in front of someone else. It taps into a common truth, which is that letting a stranger rub your naked body with oils *can* be kind of weird (or at least, it breaks a lot of the boundaries we tend to heed elsewhere in society). Mulaney could have shared this observation in a lot of ways, but he chooses to heighten his observation by exaggerating his behaviors in response to it. And he doesn't just say something like "So I took off my socks"; he uses a full reversal by actually putting on more clothes. In other words, he uses both misdirection and exaggeration.

CREATE CONTRAST

Contrast—juxtaposition between two or more elements—is another tool in your comedic toolbelt. If your observation stems from

Airplane Seating Chart

TheCooperReview.com

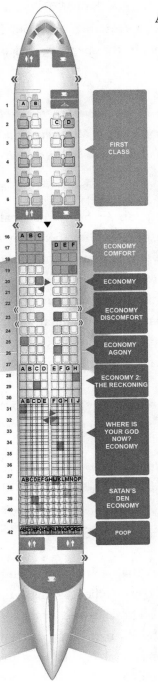

FIRST CLASS

ECONOMY COMFORT

ECONOMY

ECONOMY DISCOMFORT

ECONOMY AGONY

ECONOMY 2: THE RECKONING

WHERE IS YOUR GOD NOW? ECONOMY

SATAN'S DEN ECONOMY

POOP

LEGEND

Passenger judging you

▼ Stewardess who won't let you use the front bathroom

Screaming baby

Child kicking or banging on your headrest while trying to use the in-flight entertainment

Passenger using knee defender

Passenger leaning so far back she is in your lap

Barefoot foot fungus passenger with feet in your space

Passenger stealing your armrest while eating tuna fish and a boiled egg

Arguments on the verge of becoming all-out brawls

incongruity, some degree of contrast is likely baked in. If not, look for ways to create it! Take this commentary from Seth Meyers, building on an observation about the spending budget of the New England Patriots:

The New England Patriots have become the first NFL team to buy their own plane to fly to games . . . Meanwhile, the Cleveland Browns have been downgraded to the overhead bin on Spirit Airlines.

The Patriots have a reputation for being the wealthiest, most successful team in the league, but even for them, buying a plane is out of the norm; you might expect a team to fly first class or charter a flight, but not to own an aircraft. But notice that Seth doesn't actually exaggerate what the Patriots did to create comedy. Instead, he chooses a team with the polar opposite reputation and goes even farther outside the norms in the opposite direction, inventing an outlandish and contrasting fate for the notoriously woebegone Cleveland Browns.

Or notice how Chelsea Peretti more subtly uses contrast to talk about the pressure society puts on women versus men:

I just want to feel what it feels like to have male confidence. My fantasy of what it's like to be a guy is you wake up in the morning, and your eyes open, and you're like "I'm awesome! People probably want to hear what I have to say!"

Chelsea doesn't directly say that women are often made to feel they aren't valued, which is a truth audiences might find recognizable but depressing. Instead, she makes this point by contrasting the imagined male experience. A man might not literally think these things—they're stunningly simple—but she can make audiences aware of the things they might be missing about how their experiences might differ.

In this next-level application of the technique, her observation starts with the female perspective. She then creates contrast with an exaggerated version of the male perspective. By the time we actually hear the bit, she's dropped the female perspective entirely, merely implying the contrast.

She knows that our brains will fill in the rest.

USE SPECIFICS

If there is one thing you'll learn fast from pitching jokes in an Upright Citizens Brigade sketch writing room (aside from the fact that your teacher, Will Hines, inevitably has the best pitch every time), it's that specificity, detail, and color can take a comedic bit from good to great. Consider this joke from Jimmy Fallon:

> *British researchers are warning that one-fifth of the world's plant species are at risk of extinction. Even worse, kale is expected to survive.*

What if his punch line had been even slightly less specific? Something like "Even worse, vegetables are expected to survive." It just doesn't work quite as well, does it? That's because it's a more generic choice. The version Fallon chose—kale—is not only more specific, it also carries a slew of widely recognized and polarizing associations (e.g., hipsters, health nuts, food fads, and things that are difficult to chew).*

---

*This association even transcends species. Kanzi, a bonobo who speaks through lexigrams, dubbed kale "slow lettuce" because it takes longer to chew than other greens. To our knowledge, Fallon has not yet tested this material on Kanzi.

Maria Bamford is a master at constructing jokes with precise, vivid language:

> *I was so sick of myself asking that question of people in relationships: "How did you guys meet? Did your hands come together by accident in a garden?"*

The truth at the heart of this joke—the envy she feels toward people in happy relationships, and her disdain for sappy "how we met" stories—is something a lot of us can relate to, but that doesn't make the observation inherently funny. It's the vivid language she uses to express it, evoking a mental image straight out of a Victorian novel: two forlorn souls, unlucky in love, brought together by destiny amid a sea of rosebushes and honeysuckle. There's some fun incongruity here, too, between the scene Bamford describes and how people actually meet in the twenty-first century (that is to say, hanging out on Tinder* rather than in a garden).

MAKE ANALOGIES

Just as contrast can create humor, so can comparison. Some comedians are masters of analogy, highlighting the ridiculousness of a behavior or situation by comparing it to something totally different but equally over-the-top.

Here's Jim Gaffigan using an analogy of his observation that big families like his seem to be less common these days:

> *Big families are like waterbed stores; they used to be everywhere, and now they're just weird.*

Without the waterbed store analogy, there's no humor in this observation; Gaffigan, who grew up with five siblings and is now

---

* Aka "The Garden of Earthly Horrors."

raising five kids, might just sound like he's lamenting being outside the mainstream. The humor comes from the fact that the comparison between waterbed stores and large families is so unexpected. When your brain (with Gaffigan's help) sees a way it actually makes sense, it's a satisfying surprise.

The phrases "That's like . . ." and "It's as if . . ." can help you spot analogies and eventually create your own. Once you start listening for them, you'll notice that comedians use them all the time.

Here's Hasan Minhaj highlighting his difficulty connecting with his father by comparing him to a director with a distinctive and polarizing style:

> Every conversation with my dad is like an M. Night Shyamalan movie. It's just ninety minutes of buildup to no payoff. "That's the ending??"

And John Mulaney expressing his passionate distaste for New York subway performers playing music at him loudly and nonconsensually in a crowded, sweaty place where there is nowhere to escape:

> I've never been killed by hitmen, so I don't know what it's like in the moments just before you're killed by hitmen, but I bet it's not unlike when you're on the subway and you realize that a mariachi band is about to start playing.

Good analogies are like cantilevered bridges: difficult to construct. So if this technique doesn't come easily to you, you're not alone. When comedian and bestselling author Nils Parker worked with our students to hone their comedic chops, he shared a helpful tip: The connective tissue of an analogy is almost always the emotion or opinion the comic feels about the observation they are describing. Once you figure out that emotion or opinion, the other half of the analogy will be much easier to find.

Big families—> unusual, out of style <—Waterbeds
Cool to drive drunk—> overconfident <—Can't tie your
    shoes but think you can
Dad convos—> tedious and difficult <—Shyamalan
Loud subway performers—> sensorily assaultive <—Death
    by hit squad

In other words, to create a great analogy, start by asking yourself what you feel or think about your observation, and make it hyperspecific to you. Your audience needs to understand why you, specifically, would feel or think that way—that is, it has to be "on brand" based on what they already know about you. For those who watch a lot of Mulaney's comedy, it makes perfect sense that he (or at least his onstage persona) would experience social awkwardness with something close to the fear of death.

Then try to find something more universal to compare it to—something that's generally understood to evoke that same emotion or opinion. The "generally understood" part is key: These jokes work because most people agree that waterbeds are kind of weird and outdated, and that M. Night Shyamalan movies kinda fall apart in the third act. And most people, at least in big cities, have experienced the abject terror of a sneak subway performer attack.

In sum, to build an effective analogy, find the commonality between how *you* think or feel about the specific thing you're describing and how *most people* think or feel about the thing you're comparing it to.

FOLLOW THE RULE OF THREE

As we learned earlier in this chapter, misdirection is a core principle in comedy, which is why it's important to tee up your observation in a way that makes the listener expect something different.

Comedian and author David Nihill emphasized in a workshop with our students that one easy way to hack misdirection is to follow the **"rule of three"**: list two normal or expected elements, then add an unexpected third element. The human brain constantly looks for patterns—one of the first things we learn as children is that C comes after A and B, so when we process the first two elements (A and B), we make assumptions about where the pattern will go next (C). But if we say to a four-year-old: A . . . B . . . stung me!—we create surprise and, in turn, humor. At least for the four-year-old.

Comedians use this device frequently. Here's Amy Schumer:

Yeah! What's up, Denver?! Thank you so much for coming out to my show. This is such a big deal for me. I don't know if you guys know this, but this past year, I've gotten very rich, famous, and humble.

And Tiffany Haddish, again taking an unexpected turn on the last element:

I have finally come into my full-grown womanhood. I'm a grown-ass woman: I have survived the foster care system, I have survived homelessness, I even survived the Swamp Tour with the Fresh Prince while I was high as f*ck.

In each case, the first two items establish the pattern, and the third subverts it. In contrast, how would these look if the laugh line were buried in the middle?

"I've gotten very rich, humble, and famous."
"I have survived the foster care system, I have survived the Swamp Tour with the Fresh Prince while I was high as f*ck, I even survived homelessness."

Suddenly, the humor is less clear. When you lose the funny in the middle, you lose the misdirection, the impact, and the humor.

BUILD OUT THE WORLD

Every great joke or bit starts from a funny premise. From there, there's no limit to how far you can stretch it. Ask yourself: **If this is true, what else?** In other words, if that first funny thing you just said is true, what else follows from it? And if the second thing is true, what follows from that? Whole miniature universes can be built using this technique. Every detail provides another opportunity to heighten reality to new extremes.

In an artful example from Ellen DeGeneres's 2018 stand-up special, *Relatable*, notice how the vivid and specific world she's describing gets more absurd as the joke progresses:

> *It's been fifteen years since I've done stand-up, and when I decided to do this special, a friend of mine was at my house, and I told him: "I'm going to do stand-up again." And he said: "Really?" And I said: "Yes, why?" And he said: "Well, do you think you're still relatable?" And I said: "Yes, I do think I'm still relatable. I'm a human being." He said: "Well, I mean, your life has changed so much." And I said: "I know, but I still think I'm relatable." And anyway, just then, Batu, my butler, stepped into the library and announced that my breakfast was ready and I said: "We'll continue this conversation another time."*

> *So I'm sitting in the solarium eating my breakfast, and . . . I was on my third or fourth bite of cut pineapple that Batu was feeding me and . . . I said: "Batu, I'm not hungry, I've lost my appetite. My friend has really upset me by what he said." And he said: "Well then, I shall draw you a bath, ma'am." And I said: "You don't have to announce it all the time. Just draw the bath."*

> *So I'm sitting in the tub and I'm looking out of the window at the rose garden and . . . Tatiana was tending to the roses and, anyway I get out of the tub and Batu had forgotten to put the towel next to the*

tub. Again! So I had to do that bathmat scoot all the way across the bathroom to get to the towel. And, it's a big—You can imagine how big the bathroom is. It's like . . . [motions to a huge room]. Doing the bathmat scoot. And then I stopped, and I was like: "Oh my God . . . this is relatable."

In this final line, DeGeneres is doing something particularly clever. She's using the premise of her joke as a callback (which we'll learn about shortly). She's gotten the audience so immersed in the world she's created that we've forgotten, momentarily, why it was there. She started with a little difference, then heightened, heightened, heightened, until she could get a laugh simply by reminding the audience just how far she'd come from the original premise.

Part 3: Spontaneously Funny

Most comedians spend months or even years writing and rehearsing their bits. Obviously, few of us have such a luxury. And even once we've mastered the principles of crafting great jokes, when we use humor in the real world, we generally have to come up with it on the spot. So here are some tips worth having up your sleeve for creating spontaneous humor:

KNOW YOUR SIGNATURE STORIES

We tend to assume that comedians possess the superhuman ability to be spontaneously funny all the time. Often, they do. But also true: Many jokes that *seem* spontaneous have in fact been written, workshopped, rewritten (and re-rewritten), practiced, and told in front of countless audiences countless times. Most comedians have not just one or two but a whole catalog of bits like this in their back pocket to call on when needed.

You can do the same by starting to catalog your own signature stories. These are your go-to stories, the ones you love telling, that always get a laugh—whether at cocktail parties, in the boardroom, or to your significant other who's heard them a million times.*

Now, that's not to say you should just tell the same stories over and over. Great stories persist because they're in some way universal—not just to people, but to circumstances. So if there's a story you love telling, make sure you find ways to connect it to the situation at hand, and try not to repeat it in front of the same audience more than a couple of times, or you run the risk of sounding phony. One thing that can help is to acknowledge that you use the story a lot—"I love this story because . . ." or "Here's what I always think about . . ." If you embrace your love of the story, those around you will accept the repetition as part of your character. (And all the more reason to choose your stories wisely, since they become a part of you.)

NOTICE THE HERE AND NOW

Seth Herzog has one of the hardest jobs on the planet. Apart from performing comedy shows at traditional venues like theaters and charity events, he warms up the crowd at *The Tonight Show* with Jimmy Fallon. His job is to perform comedy for big groups of strangers—who are waiting impatiently in over-air-conditioned studios for the "real" show to start—and get them loosened up. So the man knows a thing or two about getting laughs fast.

Herzog says the single quickest path to spontaneous humor is to find something specific to *this group of people* at *this moment in time*, often by noticing the odd or incongruous things in their immediate surroundings. Which might explain why John Mulaney opened his set in the historic and ornate Radio Music Hall by looking around and commenting:

---

* In the words of Comedian David Iscoe, "This is why comedians are notoriously hard to date. If you find your special comedian is always practicing bits on you, feel free to give them a chance to practice getting heckled.

I love to play venues where if the guy that built the venue could see me on the stage, he would be a little bit bummed about it. Look at this. This is so much nicer than what I'm about to do. It's really . . . It's really tragic.

Herzog says that the goal, really, is to make the audience feel special, as if the jokes were written just for them. He recommends asking yourself, "What's funny *right now*, to *this group only?* That's the fastest and best way to get a group laughing."

USE CALLBACKS

In life just as onstage, one of the easiest ways to get a laugh is to refer back to a previous joke or funny moment that happened earlier. This device is called a *callback*. Just listen for moments of laughter, make a mental note of them, and be on the lookout for opportunities to invoke them later.

Callbacks give you a lot of bang for your buck by densely packing a wealth of meaning and context into a relatively small container.

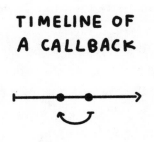

TIMELINE OF A CALLBACK

Not only that, they can promote bonding among groups. Much like good, inclusive inside jokes, callbacks play on existing relationships and knowledge, meaning that anybody who's already privy to the gag will feel special because they get to be a part of it. Back in chapter 2, we talked about how remembering moments of shared laughter reinforces connections and makes us feel more satisfied in our relationships, another reason why callbacks in general—and (inclusive) inside jokes in particular—are a potent approach for bonding groups.

It's like getting two for the price of one: People laugh at the memory of the previous joke (making you feel more connected in the process), plus you create new laughs by calling back that shared moment in a surprising or unexpected way.

Part 4: Delivering the Funny

It's showtime. For Seth Meyers, that is. Back at 30 Rock, his writers have whittled the opening monologue jokes down to a couple dozen, which he'll deliver in the upcoming dress rehearsal.

But the twelve final jokes that end up in his monologue won't necessarily be the ones that appear funniest on the page. As the great Buddy Hackett once said: "Ninety-nine percent is in the delivery. If you have the right voice and the right delivery, you're cocky enough, and you pound on the punch line, you can say anything and make people laugh maybe three times before they realize you're not telling jokes."

Below are a handful of tricks that comedians understand intuitively and utilize liberally to bring their content to life. Since they are only so useful on the page, go watch your favorite comedian in action—and if you need ideas, we've included the names of a few comedians who we think do each of these particularly well.

There is a melody and rhythm to good comedy. Consume more of it, and you'll start to learn the tune.

- **Pause before the punch.** Draw out silence to build anticipation before delivering the punch line, as the late **Mitch Hedberg** did in his sets.

- **Act it out.** Take on (and exaggerate) a character's physical behaviors, mannerisms, voice, and point of view. Watch some clips of **Sebastian Maniscalco** for an example. During his last hour special, he probably walked a half mile within a ten-foot radius of the mic stand; he kicked, he fell down, he got down on a knee . . . it looks exhausting, but it works.
- **Dial up the drama.** Heighten the emotion in your narrative by varying the pitch, tone, inflection, and pacing of your delivery. All comedians do this to some extent, but check out **Maria Bamford** for a prime example.
- **Repeat funny lines.** You'll notice that after delivering a punch line, comedians often repeat it. **Jerry Seinfeld** called that "staying in the bit." If you watch one of **Chris Rock's** comedy specials, you'll see he is a master at this.
- **Match delivery to content.** If **Tig Notaro** tried to perform Chris Rock's jokes, they wouldn't land.* Humor needs to be authentic to your content and style. Check out two different comedians and pay attention to the differences in their delivery styles.
- **Land with confidence.** Deliver punch lines emphatically. Enunciate, speak boldly, clearly, and with authority, like **Ali Wong**.

DON'T FORGET THE IMPORTANCE OF CALLBACKS

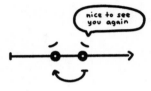

nice to see you again

---

*Except in a kind of surrealist anticomedy way, which we now realize we want more than anything to see.

Back at 30 Rock, the jokes are flying, and laughter reverberates through the halls. Seth is delivering a seemingly effortless set of brilliantly crafted, meticulously honed jokes to a studio audience, and the writers have moved on to the next day's news cycle (plus transitioned from coffee to Red Bull).

This team works tirelessly. They operate under impossibly tight timelines, react to a set of information that shifts by the minute, and deliver a product that will be viewed by millions of people.

They are in the business of comedy, but they do serious work.

And still, amid the sleepless nights, they find humor not just in the content they produce but in the *way they work*. "If we took ourselves too seriously in the office, it would be the death of comedy," Seth says.

In this chapter, we've lived in the world of comedians. And while it's easy to envision people who've devoted their lives to the craft of comedy, embedding it into their workplaces, it might be harder to imagine doing the same ourselves. But the truth is that no matter what we do or where we work, most of us can find more opportunities for humor and levity. Which is why it's time to start . . . putting your funny to work.

(*Cue page flip*)

CHAPTER 4

Putting Your

Funny to Work

"There is nothing like a gleam of humor to reassure you that a fellow human being is ticking inside a strange face."

—*Eva Hoffman*

Hear that? It's the sound of rubber meeting road. Time to dive headfirst into practical ways you can bring levity and humor to work.

But before we begin, a disclaimer: We realize that the notion of using humor in your professional life might feel overwhelming or uncomfortable. If you're having heart palpitations just thinking about the idea of trying to land a joke in front of your boss, your co-workers, or that one guy in accounting who never smiles, we encourage you to lower the bar. Remember, the goal is not necessarily to tell jokes or even be funny—it's to make more human connections during everyday moments, and to be more productive and effective (not to mention less bored) in the process.

We'll start by identifying small, tactical, and mundane ways to shift the words we use and the messages we send—minor adjustments in how we "move" that make a major difference in the way we show up in the world, and the way it shows up in return.

Next, we'll zoom out to a small set of moments that matter, exploring how acts of humor can help us navigate critical crossroads at work—whether you need to say hard things, make hard decisions, or motivate others to do—well, anything at all.

Finally, we'll shift to the interactions we have with our teams, and how strategically placed levity can help shift mindsets to unlock creative and productive work.

Communicating with Levity

Words matter. And we aren't just saying that because there are a lot of them in this book.

Research shows that the words we choose have a profound impact on our psychology and behavior. It's a principle often referred to as the Sapir-Whorf Hypothesis, which may sound like an episode of *Star Trek* but actually just means that the language we use can literally shape our cognition, our actions, and the very way we view the world. It also means that the quality of our professional relationships and the culture of our organizations are influenced directly by the way we communicate in the workplace.

Now, we're certainly far from the first to note that strong communication is mission critical for professional success. But at a time when remote work is on the rise, and digital modes of communication have all but replaced proverbial "water cooler" talk, finding ways to bond with our co-workers isn't easy. And the less we interact face-to-face, the more our written communications have to do the heavy lifting.

But many of our written communications are only doing half the job—conveying information, but failing to create human connection. We write emails that sound nothing like the way we speak, and dull our prose in ways that sound robotic and clinical. Why have so many of us bought into the belief that professional communications need to be completely devoid of personality, character, or quirk?

WHO YOU CAN BE AT WORK

perception

100%. serious

reality

100%. yourself (ok maybe 80%?)

TALK LIKE A HUMAN

People and companies everywhere are struggling with this. At Deloitte, for example, business jargon became such an issue that back in 2003, Brian Fugere, the company's then chief marketing officer, built a product to help strip the sterile jargon that had become increasingly prevalent, both internally among employees and externally between employees and clients.

The idea was born out of a mission to improve Deloitte's public image and set the company apart from all the other multi-million-dollar consulting businesses. When he first began gathering feedback from clients to help him understand what the company could be doing better, Brian expected to hear about things like industry knowledge, service offerings, and their global footprint. Instead, their primary complaint was about the consultants' style of communication. Over and over, he kept hearing a similar—and unexpected—refrain: *"So much bullshit! I wish they'd just talk straight to us."*

Deloitte consultants, like so many of us, had stopped speaking like humans. The dry, generic communication that pervaded their emails, slide decks, and other electronic media had seeped into how consultants communicated with clients and with one another. Fugere realized that he had to do something to bring humanity back to the business.

So he and his team developed software that called out the bullshit in Deloitte employees' writing. They compiled a dictionary containing all of the most objectionable jargon, holding a contest* to see who could provide the most egregious "bullwords." Among the worst offenders were "leverage," "bandwidth," "touch base," "in-

---

* The winning consultant was sent on an all-expense-paid trip to take classes at the California Academy of Tauromaquia—that is, bullfighting school.

centivize," "inoculate," "bleeding edge," "robust," "synergize," and "envisioneer." Yes, "envisioneer."

ARE YOU A ROBOT?
select all squares that contain jargon

They then wrote a program that scanned the text of an email or document and spat out a "Bull Index" score that rated the message from 1 to 10, with 10 meaning highly readable and human-sounding, and 1 meaning, well, full of bullshit.

A particularly low Bull Index score would also result in a humorous tongue-lashing, such as:

Diagnosis: you live in a rare, often irreversible state of obscurity. You are absolutely dependent on other advanced obscurists to understand anything you are trying to communicate. Sentences may be entirely devoid of dictionary-based words. Doctors at the Bull Institute would pay to study you.

The software also provided suggestions for cutting the bull. If you were found using the word "bandwidth" in a document, for example, the software flagged it as a bullword, provided helpful alternatives—like "capacity" or "time"—and then added this superfluous and ego-dismantling comment: *"Your life has come to this: you are a passive conduit for everything, kind of like a fiber optic cable. Another term that has a hint of the late 1990s tech mania."* Zing!

The software, playfully named "Bullfighter," went viral and was downloaded not only internally, but over 40,000 times externally all around the world. The results became visible almost immediately. Like a sassy librarian who lived in employees' computers, Bullfighter served as a constant (and often cheeky) reminder to stop using words that, as Fugere put it, "transform us from funny, honest and engaging weekend people into boring business stiffs."

Soon, the clarity of communications improved dramatically, sending important signals to employees and to clients. But something else important happened, too—people started to behave differently. In Fugere's words: "Bullfighter gave people in the organization the courage to take some risks and try new things. To show other people—and remind ourselves—that we are a company that has a real soul. And it signaled to the market that we were willing to do things differently, including (gasp!) things that are actually fun."

That last part is important: *doing* things that are actually fun. The change that Fugere and his colleagues experienced—in not just their language, but their *behavior*—harks back to the *Star Trek* Hypothesis. Scientists and linguists believe that words are not only a window into who we are and how we behave, they also play a role in *shaping* these things. Quite simply, if we write like corporate drones, then pretty soon we'll start acting like them, too. But people? We know how to have fun.

So how do we start making a change? First, of course, fight the bull. Whether it's face-to-face or over email, refuse to check your personality at the door.

Next, send a message that inspires others to do the same. Literally.

SEND A MESSAGE

On the day we teach this topic in our class at Stanford, we surprise our students with an activity. We have them take out their phones, go into their email Sent folder, and forward the last five (non-private) emails to their class partner. The purpose of this exercise isn't just to look for the type of corporatespeak that Bullfighter might catch—it's also to see whether the sender is providing openings for the recipient to respond with levity. As you might expect, those opportunities are few and far between.

Today's average employee spends close to 30 percent of their work hours on email and receives 120 messages per day. But online correspondence—whether on email, group chat, text, TikTok, or whatever new technology has already replaced all of these things since we wrote this sentence—doesn't need to be soul-sucking. Instead, think of digital messages as bite-sized opportunities to invite genuine connection with your co-workers and partners. Even a touch of levity can start a chain reaction that shifts the dynamic.

Below, we've outlined some of the easiest and most practical ways to incorporate levity into the messages you send. These shockingly simple techniques are perfect for turning a tedious back-and-forth into an authentic conversation.

Use Callbacks

As we learned in chapter 3, a callback references a shared experience between you and the recipient, transforming a single moment into an inside joke. Callbacks are particularly powerful because they make it easy for the other person to reply in kind. Like instant yeast when you're baking homemade bread, sprinkle some in and watch that dough rise.

One of our interviewees, Daria, shared an example from her own life. She was taking off from work early one day to get a haircut, and she and her boss, Saagar, had shared a laugh about the fact that the client deliverable she was working on might not be perfect, but at least her hair would be.

Later that evening, Daria sent the completed deliverable to her boss, along with this callback:

> *Saagar,*
> *Attached is the updated deck. Per our chat this morning, I think this will be a great tool to start the conversations we need with leadership.*
> *Let me know if the deck needs revising or if it now matches my hair: perfect.*
> *Daria*

Saagar promptly replied in kind:

> *Daria,*
> *No revisions needed, matches your hair perfectly. Enjoy the holidays with your family.*
> *With beautiful hair always,*
> *Saagar*

Just like that, Daria had reinforced the earlier moment of levity she and Saagar had shared, created a new moment, *and* made it easy for Saagar to reply in kind. Props to Saagar for not only acknowledging the levity but building on it with his sign-off.

Calling back a shared moment of any kind usually does the trick—but calling back a moment when you and the recipient laughed together, as Daria did, is particularly powerful. One colleague of ours makes a deliberate practice of this anytime she's on a call with a new client. Inevitably, a few moments of laughter arise—whether from a dog barking, conference line malfunction, or someone joking around—and she jots them in her notebook with a *star.

She doesn't go out of her way to create these moments, but she says only a small handful of calls have gone starless in the years since she started noticing. Her favorite one or two make it into her follow-up email as callbacks.

The beauty of callbacks is that they slide effortlessly into just about any part of your email. But if you're looking for a shortcut, take a page out of Saagar's book and look no farther than your trusty email sign-off.

Spice Up Your Sign-offs

Your email sign-off says a lot about you: Do you tend to end with a buttoned-up and formal "Kind regards," a mildly passive-aggressive "Thanks in advance for your help," or a jovial (and vaguely British) "Cheerio"? Sign-offs like these send subtle signals about your general affect, status, and whether you spend a lot of time in bars.

As Saagar showed, they are also prime real estate for levity. Here are a few humorous sign-offs that have caught our eye:

> When asking a favor: *With fingers and toes crossed,*
> When apologizing for an absurdly slow response: *Sheepishly,*
> When in heads-down mode: *Yours, heavily caffeinated,*
> In reference to a phone call with dog barking in the
> 　　background: *Still wondering who let the dogs out,*

Add a PS

In a series of famous studies on direct mail response, professor and author Siegfried Vögele found that 90 percent of people read the postscript before the body of the letter. Meaning that your PS is likely to be your recipient's first impression, not the last.

The same is true in email. It's like finally living out the childhood dream of dessert before dinner. As such, a PS is an impactful way to slip a little levity into an otherwise serious email. Here's an example:

> *Hey Mark,*
> *I am not sure if the hyperlink came through in yesterday's email so wanted to follow up with a low-tech, never-fail PDF with some flowcharts. Attached for your viewing pleasure.*
>
> > *Cheers,*
> > *Sachi*
>
> > *PS. PDFs are the new black.*

Hold up. Are PDFs a color? No. Does the phrase "PDFs are the new black" make sense at all? Barely. But somehow, it worked (at least well enough for Mark that he felt compelled to share it with us). What makes this technique so delightfully easy is that often a bit of randomness does the trick. Simply naming something that's true for you in the here and now, like "PS. it is HOT in Tucson" or "PS. it's raining in San Francisco" makes it clear that you're a person and not a robot (since everyone knows that robots can't function in extreme heat or rain).

Whether it's something random, a callback to the content of the email, or a reference to an inside joke you and the recipient share, a lighthearted PS is the email equivalent of a wink: It signals intimacy and invites playfulness in return.

Seize the OOOpportunity

It's one thing to bring levity to the workplace when you're actually at work, but the truly savvy know how to do it even when they're not. Crafting a memorable out-of-office reply (or OOO) is an art, and Heather Currier Hunt, Global Head of Learning & Development at IDEO, is an undisputed master of the form.

For Heather, adding levity to an OOO is "an opportunity to shift the entire auto-responder interaction from one of scarcity (nobody's home) to abundance (well, that just made my day)."

THE TYPICAL OUT OF OFFICE FORMULA

Here's an example of a typical OOO:

I am out of the office until Monday, July 10th. If you need immediate assistance, please contact . . .

Zzzzz . . . Now here's Heather's:

I am abroad with the most inconsistent wifi I have ever experienced. It's the substantiation of mindfulness, the invitation to a million moments paused in the belligerent now. I will pick up with you again on July 10th when I am back in New York where the data flows like a subterranean stream and the hours are neither here nor there. Thank you for your patience in the meantime.

Over time, Heather has received many amused (and bemused) responses to her humorous OOOs, from both close colleagues and new acquaintances. She finds that it "shifts the exchange from 'I have a request or need' to 'I see and hear you,'" thus setting the tone for a more productive dynamic once she's back online.

Don't worry, though—you don't have to go quite as all-out as Heather to infuse levity into your OOO. Anything simple, light-hearted, and human should do the trick. When a colleague of ours recently took a trip to the mountains, anyone who wrote to him during that period received this message back:

> Oh hello! I am backpacking in the Sierra Nevada without cell service through September 22. Yours will be my favorite email to respond to upon my return.
> With love (and favoritism),
> Peter

A callback within a spiced-up sign-off, a hint of exaggeration, and a whole lot of humanity.

MAKE AN IMPRESSION

Our brains make judgments astonishingly quickly—so quickly, in fact, that when researchers Nalini Ambady and Robert Rosenthal had a group of students watch a two-second video of professors they had never met and rate them on qualities like honesty, likability, competence, and professionalism, their ratings lined up with the evaluations of students who had studied with those professors for a whole semester.

While two seconds seems extreme, the impression you make during an initial meeting has been found to play a crucial role in influencing the trajectory of your relationship. Don't leave these first meetings to chance. As you prepare for the meeting, look for clues that will help you make a personal connection—about their passions, unique experiences, and if possible, their sense of humor.

For example: Daymond John loves dad jokes.

He's also a successful entrepreneur, the founder and CEO of FUBU, and an investor on ABC's *Shark Tank*—an impressive and potentially intimidating person to meet for the first time.

That's why when Billy Gene Shaw prepared for his first meeting with John, he did his research and landed on a nontraditional approach to making a first impression. In scouring John's Twitter in advance of the meeting, Shaw noticed that John had a number of posts about his love of dad jokes (like a selfie video delivering this gem: "Did you hear about the drummer that had twin daughters? He named them Anna 1, Anna 2.").

Before the meeting, Shaw bought a book with hundreds of dad jokes and read it himself—adding notes in the margins about his favorite ones. In their first meeting, he gave John the book and thanked him for his time.

Shaw's gesture made an impression. "He knew he had the goods to impress me with his knowledge of digital media in its own right," John later reflected, but "it was such a sweetly personal gesture that it couldn't help but hit home in a special way—and out of that, the two of us became friends, over this one goofy bond."

We don't always have the luxury of an in-person meeting to make an impression. After a quick Google search, people often form opinions about us before we walk into a room with them. So it's more crucial than ever that our online presence be a reflection of the impression we want to make.

Think about how many hundreds—or thousands—of people you've "met" before walking into the room with them. A lighthearted bio is like greeting them with a smile. That's what our former student Steve Reardon did when he was on the hunt for a new job.

It was 2017, and the head of a private equity firm in San Francisco was looking to hire an entrepreneur to run a new company she was about to acquire. While sifting through applications, the hiring manager came across Reardon's. His track record was impressive—years of operating experience, successful exits of prior companies, and an MBA from a prestigious institution. Also this:

> Steve Reardon is an executive manager who has worked in a wide range of businesses, including his own tech startup, a mid-sized sports retail chain, and a global banking group. He is currently the CEO of ASG MarTech, a group of digital marketing Saas companies that includes Grade.us, Authoritylabs, Social Report and Cyfe. He also founded and hosts BlindSpot, a politics and economics podcast affectionately described by his wife and two daughters as "long, boring, and utterly devoid of substance."

The change of pace in the last line caught the hiring manager's attention. It showed wit, humility, and confidence against the backdrop of his talent and fit for the role, and she decided to invite him in for a series of interviews. In Reardon's very first interview, he was asked about—you guessed it—his "long, boring podcast." He got the job.

Of course, a lighthearted bio isn't what got Reardon hired—and it won't be the one thing to determine whether you get hired either. But when you're one of hundreds or thousands of more or less equally qualified candidates, it's often the little things—like making the person on the other end of the hiring process smile—that get you through the door, which is sometimes the hardest part.

But humor simply for the sake of it won't necessarily give you an edge. So roll up your sleeves and put those comedy techniques to work on your professional bio. And as you do, keep these four tips in mind:

- **Strike the right balance.** A humorous bio should be no less impressive than a serious one. One of the biggest mistakes people make is going overboard in the levity department. When we ran a study with our students at Stanford, we found that a clever and lighthearted line or two in an otherwise already impressive bio made readers perceive the applicant (versus an applicant with the exact same bio minus the levity) as more intelligent, likable, and desirable as a colleague, plus—wait for it—better-looking. Don't downplay your accomplishments; instead, use levity to signal that you're a multidimensional person who's not only skilled and talented, but fun to be around.

- **End on levity.** Save your "punch line" until the end: No one will see it coming after a string of serious and impressive qualifications. Steve did this masterfully with the setup "affectionately described by his wife and daughters," which primed the reader to expect some sort of gushing praise about his podcasting prowess . . . and instead, ham sandwich. That is, he threw a curve ball with the decidedly nongushy descriptor "long, boring, and utterly devoid of substance." Prefrontal cortex: activated. Cookie time.

- **Choose content strategically.** Don't just grasp at anything that's funny. Use levity strategically to (a) mitigate unwanted perceptions people might have of you, and (b) showcase details that are impressive, personally important, or just plain fun to talk about but might otherwise be strange or awkward to include.

    If you meet Reardon in person, you'll quickly realize why he self-describes as a rugby-playing Aussie with a booming voice and a larger-than-life presence. He knows he can be seen as intimidating by colleagues and overconfident by potential employers. He's found that self-deprecating humor and sharing about his family makes him more relatable and allows people to see his softer side. (For the record, he loves his family non-strategically, too.)

Revealing interesting and unexpected details about yourself opens the door to a different kind of conversation. It's a lot more interesting and fun to talk about your podcast, your passion for bird-watching, or your samurai sword collection than, well, lots of other things you'll talk about instead.

- **Self-deprecate with caution.** Being self-deprecating is a smart strategy for a CEO with a killer résumé. But for someone relatively early in their career, it can be risky—especially if the subject of self-deprecation is a skill or competency relevant to the job. Think of how differently Steve's last line would land if he were applying for a job *producing podcasts*. So if you're going to self-deprecate, make it about something unrelated to your work. Our friend, Michael Kives, used the following bio when he visited our class:

Michael Kives is the founder and CEO of K5 Global, a media and financial services advisory firm. He previously worked as a motion picture agent with Creative Artists Agency, where he represented actors, singers, and world leaders including Arnold Schwarzenegger, Katy Perry, and Warren Buffett. As a high school student, Michael became the first and only person ever to win the World Debate Championship twice, thus earning the title World's Most Persuasive Teenager. He now lives in LA alone with no pets or even a plant.*

---

* We are delighted to report that Michael is now happily married, cohabitating, and still living in LA, in case you'd like to mail him and his lovely wife, Lydia, and their daughter a succulent.

By self-deprecating strategically, Kives simultaneously channeled humor and vulnerability without downplaying his professional competence.

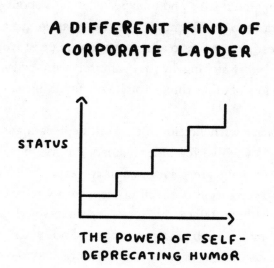

A DIFFERENT KIND OF CORPORATE LADDER

STATUS

THE POWER OF SELF-DEPRECATING HUMOR

Navigating Difficult Moments

So far, we've looked at ways to insert levity into mundane, trivial interactions. Now it's time to learn how to use it in a few of the more important moments of your professional career.

When the chips are down, our instinct is often to stay serious—after all, you don't want to come off as blithe or flippant at a time that requires sensitivity. But believe it or not, humor can help us navigate those tough pressure-cooker moments. Here are some ways workplace humor savants have used levity to say hard things, make hard decisions, and convince others to do the same in high-stakes environments:

SAYING THE HARD THING

In a perfect world, our professional lives would be easy, pleasant, and devoid of conflict. But we all know that's not the reality. When we're faced with difficult or uncomfortable conversations and inter-actions in the workplace—whether it's raising personal concerns, addressing group dynamics, or defusing an awkward situation—levity can help whatever you're saying go down a little easier.

Saving Saboteurs from Themselves

John Henry, a senior management consultant with one of the world's largest firms, advises a diverse portfolio of senior executive clients and boards. Though he's found that the social dynamics impeding productive work are often the same wherever he goes, it can be dif-ficult to broach the topic without raising his clients' hackles.

That's why he keeps a copy of the CIA's *Simple Sabotage Field Manual*, a set of guidelines devised by U.S. government officials to sabotage terrorist organizations from the inside, in his briefcase. Originally developed by the OSS during World War II, the *Simple Sabotage Field Manual* is a guide for, as the CIA puts it, "teaching people how to do their jobs badly."

Here's a sample of some of the tactics our nation's best intelli-gence officers recommend you use to undermine the operations and efficiency of a terrorist cell—or a typical American board meeting:

1. *When possible, refer all matters to committees for "further study and consideration." Attempt to make the committees as large as possible—no fewer than five people.*
2. *Make speeches. Talk as frequently as possible and at great length. Illustrate your "points" by long anecdotes and accounts of personal experiences.*
3. *Haggle over the precise wording of communications, minutes, resolutions.*

4. *Bring up irrelevant issues as frequently as possible.*
5. *Refer back to matters decided upon at the last meeting and attempt to reopen the question of the advisability of that decision.*

Now picture John Henry, sitting in a board meeting with some very important clients that he's there to advise as they unwittingly perform the very acts of sabotage that the CIA recommends using on its enemies. They're revising decisions, getting bogged down in minutiae, and burying critical decisions under layers of bureaucracy. This is an uncomfortable reality to point out, but John prides himself on voicing what his clients need to hear—not what's comfortable.

So instead of rattling off a list of all the things the company leadership is doing wrong, he whips out the *Simple Sabotage Field Manual* and proceeds to read the tips listed above. At first the executives laugh nervously in self-recognition. Then they begin laughing in earnest, as the absurdity begins to dawn on them.

It's one thing to be advised that you should probably form fewer committees. It's another to learn that you're unwittingly employing a level of sabotage endorsed by our nation's intelligence agents to wreak havoc on your own company. The sheer humor of the moment allows Henry to deliver the uncomfortable message in a way that gets people's attention and motivates change while also being easy to stomach.

Acknowledging Mistakes

For another one of our interviewees, the uncomfortable thing to acknowledge was her own mistake. Sonal Naik was in the midst of planning a daylong executive offsite for the head of product at a multinational IT company. Her client ran a $40 billion business and was convening more than twenty senior leaders for a session that she would be designing and facilitating. This was a high-stakes session with a senior crowd of executives, and with the date fast approaching, it was critical that she get her client caught up (and bought in) on the session's design.

Scheduling constraints had left her with only a thirty-minute prep call, and so with lots to cover in little time, she started talking double-speed, powering through one point after another with barely a pause to breathe. After a minutes-long monologue, Naik's client cut in, letting out an exasperated sigh and blurting, "You went too long! Sonal, you went too long!"

Naik promptly went on mute and tried not to freak out.

She took a moment to gather herself and wrapped up the call on a relatively positive note. But she recalls thinking that being admonished by her client for her long-windedness was not the ideal way to win them over on the eve of a high-stakes assignment.

So after the call ended, she sent a very short email summary of next steps to all the participants, and in lieu of the traditional "Thanks" or "Best," she ended with the sign-off "In Future Brevity, Sonal."

Naik wasn't expecting anyone to acknowledge this jab at her own expense. But to her surprise, she received responses from three other members of the client team who had been on the call and clearly appreciated the joke. One wrote, "Hah! Future brevity—nice." Another replied, "Great recap Sonal . . . definitely brief and not long :)." And a third shot back, "Loved the brief update."

When Naik met the CEO in person on the morning of the event, he shook her hand warmly and shot her a knowing smile. Later, she marveled at how that tiny gesture had defused the tension between them and established rapport after a somewhat rocky start.

Giving Tough Love

David Hornik, a general partner at the VC firm August Capital, uses humor as a tool for defusing tension when delivering tough but necessary feedback to his team and to the entrepreneurs he advises.

David recalls one board meeting at which a head of marketing described the progress he had made in driving down the cost of customer acquisition. On the surface, the numbers told a compelling story: The cost of acquiring the customer had come down 30 percent that month. However, when he looked more closely, Hornik realized that the price would have to come down another 3,000 percent in order for the cost of acquisition to be viable. Hornik couldn't let this fact go unacknowledged, but rather than embarrassing the CMO or putting him on the defensive by pointing out the unflattering math, he simply said with a smile, "Awesome, now just do that 100 more times and we'll be on to something." Everyone got the point, and they had a good chuckle at the same time—even the CMO.

Of course, it's not always best to make light of things that are uncomfortable (as we'll explore later on), but according to Hornik, humor "eases the blow" of hard feedback when it's employed thoughtfully. While negative criticism might make the recipient defensive or resistant, "thoughtful joking," says Hornik, can "deliver that same message without making it feel so bad."

Or, in the words of Mary Poppins, the original lifestyle guru: "A spoonful of sugar helps the medicine go down."

Saying Goodbye

What is it about saying goodbye that makes us so uncomfortable? We make sneaky Irish exits from parties, we avoid talking about death (the Big Goodbye), and we'd often rather ghost someone (translation for nonmillennials: the slow fade) than acknowledge the spark is going out.

The workplace is often no different. But how you say goodbye when you leave a job makes a lasting impression. A psychological principle called the **Peak-End Rule** explains that the moments people remember most from an experience are the most emotionally heightened one and the final one. Which means that after you're gone (from the job, that is) people are most likely to recall two key things: that one big exciting project you worked on, and how you said goodbye.

Most goodbye notes follow a similar formula:

Today is my last day at _____. Over the last _____ years, I have had the pleasure and privilege of working with many of you. I have so enjoyed my time at _____ working alongside so many kind and talented people and am so grateful for all that I have learned. I hope our paths will cross again.

Yawn.

If you've been working with these people in any capacity (which we assume you have, unless you're a remote worker without access to cellular service or Internet), we *know* you have something more personal to say to your co-workers than "I hope our paths will cross again."

Between the countless hours spent on video conference calls, all the awkward elevator rides, and the impromptu conversations while unjamming the printer, you should have ample seed material to mine for a callback or reference to some unique quirk of your office culture. A goodbye note can be sincere and heartfelt while also making people smile, as in this lighthearted goodbye email from an intern who recently left her post at a large book publisher:

Hi all,

As everyone probably already knows from the donuts this morning, today is my last day. This summer has been a whirlwind for me— my previous job titles have included Ski Boat Driver and Cat Sitter, but this has been my most important undertaking. So from the bottom of my heart, thank you for taking me on, for involving me in your projects, and for answering all of my questions, no matter how annoying! Thank you for lending me your odd passwords, for letting me sit in on your meetings, and for making me feel included here every day. (And thank you for the donuts.) I appreciate every bit of it, and each one of you. In an hour, I'll have to turn in my badge and head home to start packing, but I hope you'll stop by my cubicle after I'm gone—I've left some stuff there for everyone. Some of it is edible.

Gratefully,

Kate

We can all make endings a little less painful—and leave a lasting positive impression—by leaning into goodbyes with levity and humanity.

PERSUADING OTHERS

While there are innumerable situations in the workplace that qualify as high-stakes, one that can be particularly pivotal is making "the ask": that moment when you want (or need) something from someone, and it's up to you to persuade them to give it to you. Sometimes humor can be just the thing to punch up your persuasive powers and get whatever it is you're after.

Getting Your Foot in the Door

That was the case for Sara Blakely, the founder and CEO of the wildly popular foundation garment manufacturer Spanx. In the early days of Spanx, Blakely faced a significant challenge: getting prominent retailers to carry her product in their stores. She admits it was not an easy sell. Spanx was a new product from an unknown brand entering a crowded market. Oh, and the most common misspelling of the brand's name redirected to a porn site.

With limited funds and even more limited connections, she had no choice but to pick up the phone and start cold-calling. She went down the list—Neiman Marcus, Nordstrom, Saks Fifth Avenue, Bloomingdale's, QVC—but no one would return her calls. Sara was convinced that all she needed was five minutes on the phone with a buyer to sell her product. But this was easier said than done.

So in a moment of inspiration, she bought a few pairs of shoes, went to the post office, and mailed each of them a shoebox containing a single high heel and a handwritten message that read "Just trying to get my foot in the door. Can I have a few minutes of your time?" followed by her phone number.

It worked. The buyer at Neiman Marcus was so amused by the gag that he actually called her back. The ensuing deal they made gave her legitimacy, which helped her build relationships with other big retailers. Within a year, Blakely had accounts with every store on her initial list—and more.

Naming the Elephant

Over the course of a decades-long career that spans the early days of Silicon Valley, Apple, venture capital, and numerous boards of directors, Heidi Roizen has often been the only woman in a room full of men. Early in her tenure on the board of a public technology company, Roizen found herself dealing with a delicate problem during meetings: Every time a group would return from a break, she'd realize that her colleagues had been continuing discussions—and even making decisions—in the men's room.

As Roizen describes her dilemma, she wanted to shine light on the gender dynamics at play and get the men to stop discussing things in the (damn) bathroom. So one day, as the board left the meeting room for a break, she said simply, "If you guys continue this conversation in the men's room . . . I'll come in."

Her approach was simple, lighthearted, disarming—and successful. Roizen says that the line got a laugh, and that her colleagues made the change she wanted. She got her point across in a way that addressed the issue tangentially and without pointing fingers, shedding light on the problem without forcing her colleagues to look directly into the sun.

Asking (and Re-Asking)

Making an ask is hard. Making an ask and getting a yes is even harder. If you want something from someone—whether it's the shelf space you need to launch your product, a valuable connection, or a little bathroom break consideration—chances are that your ask isn't the only one in their metaphorical in-box.

Now, we're sure you've heard the advice that when making an ask, it pays to offer *them* something of value: knowledge, a fancy fruit basket, your pet frog,* whatever. Believe it or not, a laugh might be just the thing.

We don't often think of laughter as something we can *give*, but it is. People—especially powerful people—so often react to "asks" by shutting off, as a defense mechanism to protect themselves and their time. But giving the gift of laughter—or even just a smile— opens them up in ways that heirloom papaya from Belize can't.

This principle holds just as true when you've already made the ask and it's time for a nudge. You've likely experienced that mild sense of self-loathing that bubbles up when sending emails that start with lines like "Hi, just following up on . . . ," "Hey there, just checking on the status of . . . ," or "Sorry to nudge, but . . ." It can be painful for both sides. But it doesn't have to be.

A while back, an interviewee of ours, Rebecca, got ghosted. Not in the dating app sense, but in a sense that was more financially problematic. She had recently done some freelance work for a former colleague, and her invoice had gone unpaid for months. So she sent a reminder. Crickets. She nudged, politely, via both email and text. No reply. Weeks passed, and she sent another nudge. No dice.

---

*If you got this deep-reach callback to the negotiations study in chapter 2, we are proud of you.

After months of no contact, she texted the former colleague a single image:

Where multiple heartfelt entreaties had failed, a cute (desperate) cat and some Adele lyrics saved the day. The woman replied in a matter of minutes, and a few weeks later, the money was in Rebecca's account.

The lesson is obvious: A funny or lighthearted nudge will often get a reply faster than one that's polite and bland. It doesn't have to be hilarious, brilliant, or even cat-related*—it just has to let the levity do the work.

Shifting Mindsets and Unlocking Creativity on Teams

Now that we've covered communicating with levity and navigating difficult moments, it's time to look at how levity, when deployed strategically, can help shift mindsets to unlock creative and productive work on teams.

---

*Though if you do decide to throw a cat at your problems, it'll land on them with all four feet.

BREAKING THE ICE

When we show up for a workshop, an offsite, or any other gathering where intense work needs to take place, we often enter the room distracted. We're thinking about who's on drop-off duty for our kids the next morning. We're worrying about a loved one who's sick. We're thinking about the groceries being delivered at five o'clock—we *are* going to be home by then, right?

That's why it's vital that the first few moments of our gatherings clear away those distractions: The way we kick things off can have an outsized and reverberating influence on the group dynamic for the remainder of the time we spend working together. Starting a work session with levity is a powerful way to establish a positive mindset, break us out of established habits and mental patterns (at least temporarily), and ensure that everyone is primed for their best work.

Now, when we talk about starting off a group work session with humor, your mind probably goes straight to one place: the dreaded icebreaker. If you've spent any time in the corporate world, you've probably been subjected to lots of these—the Human Knot, Two Truths and a Lie, "If you were a fruit, what would you be?" But breaking the ice doesn't have to be tedious, cheesy, or overwrought. And it's also not the only way that levity can help prime people for good work.

In general, the levity savants we spoke with used tactics that fall into three major categories: the traditional icebreaker (with caveats), the tone setter, and the cold open. To illustrate the first two examples, let's travel to a conference hall in Napa, where one of the Two Stephens is hard at work. . . .

The Icebreaker

One warm August morning in Napa, NBA star Stephen Curry convened an offsite for his new business venture, SC30 Inc. It was a company that he and his good friend, college teammate, and business partner Bryant Barr had created to expand Curry's brand off the court and into the arenas of brand partnerships, media, investment, and philanthropy.

Representatives from more than twenty of SC30's strategic partners filed into a bright, sunny conference hall, not sure what to expect. Curry's idea was simple but disruptive: Rather than meet with each of his new partners separately, he'd bring them all together in one place to identify opportunities for collaboration across SC30's ecosystem. Participants included leaders of major global companies (Rakuten, Callaway, Under Armour), portfolio company founders SC30 had invested in, Curry's personal board of advisors, and a small number of trusted family members and friends.

The nervous excitement in the room was palpable as they waited for Curry to arrive. Everyone wanted to make a good impression on everyone else—and especially on the larger-than-life leader who had gathered them together.

Luckily, SC30 president Bryant Barr had something planned to loosen everyone up: an icebreaker that was personal, relevant to the work they'd be doing, and—of course—designed to create moments of shared laughter.

Barr had everybody in attendance pick a partner, then asked them all a series of questions that ranged from "What's one time in your life when you were underrated?" to "What's your best relationship advice or marriage tip?"* As Barr read the questions aloud, each duo had sixty seconds to give each other their answers before switching to a new partner at the sound of a bell.

It was lively, chaotic, and unexpected, and before long the room was full of energetic conversation and laughter. As the icebreaker

---

* A prompt that was passed to Naomi by friend and former colleague Saagar Thakkar, who uses it in his innovation sessions. If you're looking for relationship advice, Saagar has a treasure trove.

came to a close, everybody was feeling far more comfortable with one another and ready to get to work.

The traditional icebreaker gets an undeservedly bad rap—and sure, some of them can be a little frivolous (see: fruit)—but when designed thoughtfully, icebreakers act as social lubricant, bringing out vulnerability, honesty, and intimacy. The best icebreakers provide that sought-after balance between gravity and levity, sparking laughter while also grounding people in the important goals of the day.

But despite what their name implies, icebreakers aren't the only way to break the ice. Good leaders know how to prime their people through simple actions and gestures that set the tone they're after.

The Tone-Setter

Stephen Curry knew the value of setting the right tone that day in Napa. Participants may have been more loosened up than when they walked in, but their backs stiffened in their chairs as Curry made his way to the front of the room. They had become more comfortable with one another, but they still weren't quite sure how to act around him.

As he made the kind of heartfelt, gracious opening remarks one might expect to kick off such an event, the crowd nodded and half-smiled at the appropriate intervals . . . but a low hum of nervous energy still pervaded the room. Apparently, Curry could feel it, too. So after wrapping up his remarks, instead of retreating to the back of the room, he announced, "I'd like to conclude with my favorite Steve Ballmer* impression."

People looked around, confused.

Without skipping a beat, Curry puffed up his chest and bellowed "WHO'S FIRED UP TO BE HERE?!?!? I'M FIRED UP!!!!!! I'M

---

* If you don't get this reference: Pause. Google "Steve Ballmer going crazy on stage." Watch the video of the former Microsoft CEO. Return to book.

FIRED UP TO BE HERE! IF YOU AREN'T FIRED UP, IT'S YOUR FAULT!! WHO'S FIRED UP??!!"

Just like that, the tenor of the event completely shifted. The room exploded with laughter, through dropped jaws and incredulous looks. Everyone instantly relaxed back into their chairs, their polite, closed-lipped smiles morphing into genuine grins. By dropping a formal facade and totally committing to silliness, Curry raised the energy in the room, and with it, the potential for what the group might accomplish. He made it clear that this was a space where they didn't have to take themselves too seriously, even though they were there to get serious work done.

As Curry showed, breaking the ice doesn't always come in the form of a formally structured activity—sometimes it can be a matter of sending the right signals. Humans are social creatures; we're inclined to mirror the highest-status individual in our midst, which means that leaders can keep things light and create the conditions necessary for good work by walking the walk.

The Cold Open

There's a third way to set a tone with levity: an advanced form of icebreaker called the "cold open." Cold opens are attention-grabbing, memorable, and often the favored tool of professional facilitators.

One such professional is Chris Ertel, a social scientist, strategic conversation designer (a title he invented for the work he does), and coauthor with Lisa Kay Solomon of the book *Moments of Impact*. One of Ertel's all-time favorite cold opens is one he designed called the Backwards Bicycle, drawing on the viral video by engineer Destin Sandlin.

Backwards Bicycle involves a bicycle that works just like a normal bike, except when you turn the handlebars to the right, the wheel turns to the left, and when you turn the handlebars to the left, the wheel turns to the right. You'd think that learning to ride this contraption would be a pretty simple thing to figure out, given that we all know how to ride a bicycle.

It's not. Here's how the cold open works: The participants are convened at the start of the session, where a backwards bicycle sits at the front of the room. Ertel holds out a helmet and challenges a volunteer to ride the bike from one end of the stage to the other. Inevitably, the volunteer tries and fails. Once the laughter dies down, he pauses the exercise. "We must have a knowledge gap at play," he explains. "You can't ride the bike because I haven't given you the *information* you need." So he explains in greater detail how the bicycle works. The volunteer nods, confident, ready to give it another go. She's got this!

But she hasn't got this. A new volunteer is called, and of course he's no more successful than the first.

Ertel again pauses the exercise and feigns confusion: "You have all the information you need—you know how to ride the bike in this new way. So what we have here must be a problem of *motivation!* I haven't incentivized you adequately." And with that, Ertel reaches into his pocket and pulls out $200 in $20 bills. Eyes widen. "Who'd like to give it a try now?"

One after another, grown men and women climb onto a bicycle and wobble about on the stage, some even toppling over. They're so determined, and they try all kinds of different techniques. Some even try to cheat. Meanwhile, the room is full of laughter.

This might sound like some kind of sadistic hazing ritual, but in reality, the Backwards Bicycle is designed to illuminate a principle central to what he has been tasked with convening this group to tackle. It demonstrates, quite simply, that change is hard—even if we know *how* we need to change, and even if we're *motivated* to change.

In his debrief, Ertel thoughtfully harvests reflections from the group to weave together the story he knows they will tell. Deeply ingrained patterns of thinking, behavior, and process underlie the challenge of the day—and this group cannot expect their triumphant ride into the sunset to come without sustained commitment and setback. The message is: The work starts today but extends long beyond it. This metaphor grounds and contextualizes the day's work—creating laughter along the way.

SPARKING CREATIVE IDEAS

Before we leave you, we'd be remiss not to talk about the powerful effects of levity when the task at hand is coming up with new ideas.

Humor encourages a kind of mental gymnastics that reveals connections, patterns, and interpretations we'd previously missed. It widens our perspective, makes us feel psychologically safe, and creates fertile ground for creativity to thrive. In the wise words of the Dalai Lama, "Laughter is good for thinking because when people laugh, it is easier for them to admit new ideas to their minds."

For a closer look at exactly *how* you can harness levity to spark creativity in practice, let's explore a few favorite examples from our interviewees. They demonstrate two different approaches to incorporating levity into the brainstorming process—first tangentially, and then directly.

The Bad Idea Brainstorm

Astro Teller is a computer scientist, entrepreneur, and AI pioneer who heads X—the research and development facility formerly known as Google X and often referred to as the Moonshot Factory. Teller's organization is a diverse group of inventors and entrepreneurs who create new technologies aimed at improving the lives of millions, even billions, of people. Their mission is to tackle the world's most intractable problems, with the speed and ambition of a startup. In short: They create radical new technologies to solve some of the world's hardest problems.

As such, a robust and hyperproductive process for unlocking bold and novel ideas is crucial to the organization's success. One of the most effective approaches Teller has found is an unlikely one: He challenges them to come up with *bad ideas.*

"If I say, 'Go brainstorm good ideas,'" says Teller, "then people will think, 'Oh, God, everything I say has to be a good idea.'" Using the word "good," he says, puts limits on the way his team thinks. But if he specifically requests "the silliest, stupidest ideas," people often come up with crazier—and often better—solutions. These brainstorms are full of ludicrous ideas and raucous laughter, but they also yield brilliant results.

It's only by freeing ourselves from the pressure to be "normal" or serious, Teller explains, that we're able to unlock our most creative selves. He says that there's "a voice in your head that says 'Don't say silly things'"—but that when your brain censors your silliest thoughts, it's also censoring your most brilliant ones. "There are no genius ideas that don't sound crazy at first."

Try it yourself by holding a "Bad Idea Brainstorm." Instead of just assuring your team that "there are no bad ideas," explicitly ask for the silliest, craziest, worst possible ideas they can think of—the ones they think have no chance of actually working. In the process, you'll shift the energy of the room, set orthodoxies aside, get some good laughs along the way, and maybe even find a few unexpectedly brilliant solutions.

Pitches from the Pros

In 2017, a global retailer was facing an existential crisis to their business: Growing competition from online channels meant rapidly declining foot traffic in their stores.* Business as usual wasn't working, and they needed fresh ideas, fast. So their creative agency's strategy team reached out to an unexpected partner: Matt Klinman.

Klinman is the former head writer for *The Onion* Video and the CEO of Pitch, a comedy writing app that started at *Funny or Die.*

---

*Giving new (and negative) meaning to the phrase "reduce your footprint."

Pitch is like a giant writers' room on the Internet, where thousands of comedy writers come together to hone their craft, sell some jokes, and, as Klinman says, "enable each other."

You've likely read many of the pitches their comedians have written for a range of brands they work with, from tweets to marketing copy to television commercials.*

A few years ago, Klinman found that many of his clients were interested in using Pitch for something completely different: to uncover valuable insights into their products, their audience, and their messaging. Because, as we know, inside every joke is an intrinsic truth about everyday life, and comedians are some of the world's experts at mining the world for those truths.

So when the agency strategists approached Klinman with the challenge at hand—*How should stores compete against e-commerce?*—the first thing Klinman did was turn it into a joke setup: *Reasons It's Better to Go to the Store than Buy Online.* He posted it on Pitch, and hundreds of writers immediately got to work.

Pretty soon, punch lines came rolling in, from "Amazon never lets you keep the hanger" to "We don't have a Sbarro at home" to "Because my New Year's resolution was to meet new people." In just a few hours, Klinman and the agency strategists had generated hundreds of jokes ranked by how funny they were.

But underlying each of these jokes was real insight. "Amazon never lets you keep the hanger" tapped into the reality that little extras go a long way. "We don't have a Sbarro at home" reminds us that people love to shop and snackers love food, something they can't instantly get online. And "Because my New Year's resolution was to meet new people" taps into the fact that online shopping is

---

* And then there are the topics the writers just pitch to one another for fun— like "Oddly Specific Things to Be Insecure About." Responses to that one included "My cat only meows at my boyfriend," "I can never flip a pancake on the first try," and "My ears are too small to hold a cigarette." Did you just check your own ears? So did we.

a solitary activity—and into the real desire for in-person connection in an increasingly disconnected world.

Klinman's agency partners mined the jokes for these real insights. The process of generating jokes, rather than simply ideas or solutions, inspired a creative new in-store customer experience strategy that included elements drawn directly from the jokes, like reconfiguring the store's layout to encourage more face-to-face interaction.

There's nothing stopping you from doing this yourself, with your own team. Want to get the creative juices flowing? Just create a challenge question (as the agency strategists did), turn it into a joke setup (the way Klinman did), and have team members write their joke pitches on Post-it Notes. Collect their Post-its and put them on the board anonymously—then enjoy the content and start grouping by real-world theme. (Hint: encourage them to read chapter 3 beforehand to prime their comedic superpowers. We recommend this for outcomes, not just book sales.)

And if you're serious about jump-starting creative thinking on your team, you should seriously consider bringing in professional comedians.

Comedians are uniquely talented at finding the nuanced truths hidden away in the nooks and crannies of life—it's what they do every day. (And if you don't know any comedians, just reach out; we know a bunch!)

* * *

Whether you're trying to shift your team's mindset or just write a better LinkedIn bio, levity and humor are essential tools for forging more human connections and improving performance, strengthening bonds in the good times, and fostering resilience for the bad times. While not every situation is the right time to elicit laughter, hopefully we've provided you with a litany of ways to punctuate your workday grind with a little more joy.

CHAPTER 5

Leading

with Humor

"If you're leading and no one is following, you're just taking a walk."

—John Maxwell

One **brisk fall** evening in 2009, bareMinerals founder and CEO Leslie Blodgett sat in her kitchen with a notebook, a cup of Earl Grey, and an idea. She jotted down some impromptu notes and took another sip.

Leslie's company was a pioneer in the mineral makeup and skincare product space, and it had taken off in a big way mostly thanks to word-of-mouth marketing from satisfied customers. But business had slowed amid one of the worst economic recessions in U.S. history, and, as Blodgett put it, "I wanted to help women feel beautiful even when the economy was ugly."

So she decided to take out a full-page ad in *The New York Times*. Now, most CEOs releasing such a costly and high-profile piece of copy would have leaned on a team of copywriters, consulted a brand strategist, or outsourced to a PR department.

Not Blodgett.

The notes she jotted down that evening came from the heart. They were imbued with authenticity, vulnerability, and, yes, levity. After a few back-and-forths with a graphic designer, she sent it to the *Times:*

The advertising experts tell us that people don't read lots of copy.

I really hope not because this cost a fortune.

MAYBE YOU'VE HEARD OF US. IF YOU HAVE, IT'S MOST LIKELY BECAUSE SOMEONE TOLD YOU ABOUT US. We aren't the type to swing from chandeliers to get noticed (although we do have a fondness for chandeliers—they appear in every one of our boutiques). You also won't find us hiring celebrities to speak for us. Don't get us wrong, we love famous people, but we just don't feel we need to pay them to talk about our products.

Back to the reason for this letter. WE ARE THE PEOPLE BEHIND bareMinerals, THE GREATEST MAKEUP ON THE PLANET. WOMEN OFTEN TELL US THAT OUR PRODUCTS HAVE CHANGED THEIR LIVES. We love hearing this and believe it based on all the awesome emails we receive.

WE ARE PRETTY MUCH EXPERTS ON THE SUBJECT OF SKIN. OUR FOUNDATION IS THE MOST POPULAR PRODUCT OF THEM ALL. IT HAS WON A GAZILLION AWARDS, AND MILLIONS OF WOMEN USE IT. We're really proud of our products and how they perform. If you want a foundation that gives you stunning skin and feels like your bare skin— bareMinerals is for you.

We do love our products, but we love our customers more. This note is also a big thank you to all the women that believe in us. It's all about keeping it real, sharing stories and meeting with women one-on-one at our boutiques, Sephora, Ulta, and some department stores. We think if you try bareMinerals for yourself, you will be amazed at how really incredible it is. If you don't believe us, ask someone you know. In fact, we've found that many dental hygienists use our products. Next time you're getting your teeth cleaned, just ask her.

Anyway, we just wanted to tell you that we're here, WE HAVE THE BEST PRODUCTS FOR YOUR SKIN, and we really care about making women happy. Thanks for reading this long thing. My husband was convinced you wouldn't read this far (and he's not even an ad exec).

And if you're ever in San Francisco, maybe we can chat over a cup of coffee. I'm not kidding. Call our main office line at 415-489-5000. Generally Hilda answers the phone.

Lots of Love,

Leslie
xox

Leslie Blodgett
CEO OF BARE ESCENTUALS

During a difficult time for the business, Leslie put the company's spirit—as well as her own—on full display and connected not only with customers, but with employees. As she recalls, "It was a tough economic period, and there was lots of instability and mistrust. [The ad] reduced the tension that was everywhere. It was so basic and nonprofessional that it was endearing and real." For her, injecting levity into the mix was not only natural, but crucial. "In times of uneasiness, humor becomes even more unexpected," she explains. "So when it appears, people run, not walk, towards it."

Or—if there's a phone number—they call it.

The number on the ad really did go straight to Hilda, who sat in the office lobby, where everyone passing by could hear her assuring incredulous callers that yes, the number in the ad was real, and yes, they really could schedule a coffee date with her. It was a daily reminder of what the company was really about, and of the unexpected and yet somehow pitch-perfect business decision their founder had made. Not only did her wit and warmth impact customers' attitudes toward bareMinerals, her team felt meaningful impact internally: "Yes, we sold more products—but we measured the effectiveness of that ad by the camaraderie," Blodgett says. "It was a living and very public example of our values. And the closeness we all felt made us stronger."

* * *

There are many books far better and broader than this one about how to lead. This chapter is about how to lead with humor—building on the tools we've spent the previous chapters exploring, and showing how they've come to life for a small set of remarkable leaders.

What follows isn't so much a playbook as a series of vignettes, each boiling down to one central premise: By channeling their unique sense of humor, leaders can better unite, persuade, motivate, and inspire—and, ultimately, be the kind of people that others want to follow. We hope they inspire you to do the same.

In Leaders We (Must) Trust

Before we return to story time, it's important to understand the state of affairs when it comes to modern leadership—and why it's time to rethink the way we lead.

In the quaint days of yore (it's a storytelling chapter; we're leaning in), inspirational leaders reigned as a rarefied breed possessing some unique combination of intelligence, bravery, charisma, moral superiority, and cunning resolve. Ernest Shackleton drifted on sheets of ice for months to courageously rescue his stranded crew from the

Antarctic sea. Henry Ford reinvented transportation and made the automobile affordable for middle-class families nationwide. Marco Polo traveled across the mountains of Asia and inspired generations of children to venture blindly across swimming pools.

But the days of the mythic and infallible leader are behind us.[*]

In the wake of shocking events like the Enron scandal in 2001, the U.S. subprime mortgage crisis in 2008, the Fukushima nuclear disaster in 2011, and the more recent revelation that Boeing rushed a poorly designed 737 upgrade to market, with disastrous results, our collective trust in leaders has been severely dented, if not totaled.

This degradation of trust in leadership has firmly implanted itself in the minds of employees, too: A 2019 *Harvard Business Review* survey found that 58 percent of employees trust a complete stranger more than their own boss.

Pause. Read that sentence again.

Your employees trust a *stranger* more than you!

THE OPPOSITE OF STRANGER DANGER

58% of employees trust a stranger more than their boss

Thankfully it's 5 o'clock somewhere

---

[*] Except for Oprah. She is in front of us, and she is perfect.

In worse news, 45 percent of them cited their lack of trust in leadership as the single biggest issue impacting their performance at work.

And you (leaders) seem to agree: 55 percent of CEOs believe that this crisis in confidence is a threat to your organization's growth. And you aren't wrong to worry. Lack of trust impacts your employees' motivation and productivity, the likelihood that they'll jump ship for a new company, and how much time you (and everyone else) spend frantically putting out fires that could have been avoided had your people felt comfortable discussing sensitive issues with you. (Versus a stranger they met on the bus.)

Today's business leaders find themselves tied with elected officials as the least trustworthy individuals in the eyes of eighteen to twenty-nine-year-olds: According to a 2018 Pew Research Center survey, only 34 percent of these young adults trust corporate and political leaders (who fare only slightly better among the thirty-to-forty-nine demographic). This is less than the percentage of Americans who own dogs (44 percent), meaning that in the trustworthiness power-rankings, powerful humans are losing to domesticated wolves.

This is bad, leaders.

If this makes you want to down a bottle of wine and binge watch *Golden Girls* at your next leadership offsite, rest assured: There is good news, and we have a plan. Because while trust in leadership is plunging, those organizations that somehow manage to maintain a high trust environment are thriving.

There is a volume of research that links high-trust organizations to innovation and performance. For example, the 2016 HOW Report[*] concluded that employees who work in high-trust environ-

---

[*] The 2016 HOW Report analyzed responses from 16,000 employees in 17 countries across all major industries and occupations and was independently validated by the Center for Effective Organizations at the University of Southern California. This is not funny, but it is true. (And HOW!)

ments are 32 times more likely to take risks that might benefit the company, 11 times more likely to see higher levels of innovation relative to their competition, and 6 times more likely to achieve higher levels of performance compared with others in their industry.

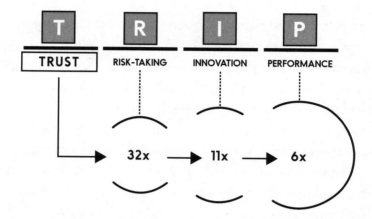

So how can today's leaders inspire trust in their employees? A 2019 survey asked employees just that; the top responses—like "knowing the obstacles the leader overcame to be successful" and "speaks like regular people"—told a consistent story: Today's employees yearn for leaders who are less mysteriously brilliant and more authentically relatable. Aspirational, yes—but not without flaws.

In short, it used to be that leaders were revered; now they need to be understood.

In a sense, this reflects a broader trend in a social-media-obsessed society. We've become accustomed to real-time updates, we crave raw and unfiltered content, and we're delighted by behind-the-scenes access to the private lives of celebrities, athletes, executives, and stars of the Puppy Bowl. Anything less than full transparency can signal "something to hide."*

---

* Roll film: *The Inventor: Out For Blood In Silicon Valley.*

Leslie Blodgett understood this when she published her ad. In fact, these were lessons she had learned (albeit serendipitously) early in her career.

Long before she could afford paid marketing (much less full-page ads in *The New York Times*), and at a time when her brand wasn't well known enough for traditional distribution, Leslie discovered the cheapest way to reach consumers was by appearing live on the home shopping television channel QVC.

For Blodgett, it was terrifying; there was no luxury of multiple takes or do-overs when the cameras were rolling. But whether she intended it or not (hint: she did not), going on QVC allowed Blodgett to showcase her authentic, unfiltered personality, including her self-deprecating, slightly unorthodox sense of humor.

Like how she'd kick off her shoes midway through a broadcast because her feet were killing her. Or how she'd take breaks from selling products to parent her son through the television (*"Trent, go to bed. I know you're watching. Turn off the TV and brush your teeth. I'm not joking, kiddo, I'll wait."*). Or how she'd tell the cameras to "stop with the closeups."

On one occasion Blodgett spun a hula hoop and played the harmonica at the same time. She wore a bikini top over her dress to talk about summer makeup. All live. On air.

And once, midway through a broadcast, when Blodgett realized her shoulder pad had migrated down to her elbow, she broke out in giggles so fierce that they almost had to cut to commercial. The show's host made Blodgett look her in the eyes in an attempt to stop the giggling. But the producer waved her off: The phones were on fire with orders.

As Blodgett watched sales of bareMinerals products take off, she realized that her authenticity and levity—quirks, imperfections, and all—struck a chord with her customers and employees.

After QVC, Blodgett never looked back. "I found that people appreciate the real," she told us. "When people have a choice—

whether it's about where to work or what products to buy—they want to know and trust who you are as a person. A sense of humor is at the center of this. It's hard to trust a person or a company that takes itself too seriously."

Everyone wants a more pleasant, more respected manager, yet the perceived lack of these traits in our leaders is contributing to a crisis of retention: A 2018 Gallup study found that nearly *50 percent* of Americans have left a job to "get away from their manager" at some point in their career.

At a time when employee turnover has increased 88 percent over the last decade, costing companies billions, the impact of humor on employee perceptions and retention is a timely salve to a silent crisis affecting leaders and organizations worldwide.

"Plus," adds Blodgett, "who *doesn't* want to work in a place that values humor and laughing and being your real self?"

Levity in Diplomacy

Many of the most compelling, memorable anecdotes we gathered in our research about leaders effectively applying levity involved high-stakes, crucial conversations—those dicey interactions when tensions (and cortisol) have been running high and traditional approaches have fallen short.

The year was 1998. United States Secretary of State Madeleine Albright was preparing for the ASEAN Summit in the Philippines—a biannual meeting hosted by the members of the Association of Southeast Asian Nations where prominent world leaders assembled to address global issues and strengthen cooperation across nations.

Secretary Albright was not particularly keen on attending—not only because ASEAN had recently and controversially accepted Myanmar as a member (a decision that the United States had strongly opposed on account of severe repression by their military government), but also because one of the diplomatic duties she was being asked to perform was . . . a skit.

Yes, the secretary of state was going to perform a skit.

As one of Secretary Albright's colleagues at the State Department had explained, it is tradition that during the formal dinner gala on the final evening of the summit, every delegation presents some kind of entertainment, usually in the form of a skit. Highlights in the years since have included South Korean foreign minister (and later secretary-general of the United Nations) Ban Ki-moon singing ABBA songs in a green sequined jacket and Russian foreign minister Sergei Lavrov appearing as *Star Wars* villain Darth Vader. These delegates do not mess around.

And as Secretary Albright's colleague explained: "The United States always does very badly." Then (we swear, this really happened) he handed her the lyrics to "Mary Had a Little Lamb."*

That year, the Russians were also performing a skit, but according to Secretary Albright, "theirs wasn't very good either." Her counterpart in the Russian government (which had historically been more supportive of Myanmar, adding to the tensions between the two delegations) was a man named Yevgeny Primakov. Just months earlier, during their first meeting, Primakov had attempted to intimidate Albright by reminding her of his former role as a senior official in the KGB. "Given my background," he said, "you *do* know that I know *everything* about you, yes?" Not the warmest start.

But with both parties in need of theatrical reinforcements, Albright, Primakov, and their associates decided—in the midst of these critically important meetings—to do something unprecedented.

They would sing a duet.

"So the night before this dinner," Albright recalls, "we all went

---

* In the words of Secretary Albright during her visit to our class: "There are things that you cannot imagine a secretary of state is ever asked to do."

to the General MacArthur suite, and the Russians brought a lot of vodka, and we rehearsed." Late into the night. Until they finally had something to perform.

The next day was long and full of difficult meetings. "Our delegations had a rumble," as Albright recalls. "And then I came out singing." Literally. Albright, the most senior dignitary representing the most powerful country in the world, regaled the throngs of foreign statesmen with her rendition of "Maria" from *West Side Story* as part of a brilliantly crafted duet in a performance they called *East West Story*. Moments later, she was joined by Primakov, who belted out "Madeleine Albright, Madeleine Albright, I just met a girl called Madeleine Albright."

And that's how "something that was going to be a disaster," as Albright put it, "turned out to be a lot of fun."

Of course, this wasn't just about fun (or vodka). Secretary Albright had used humor as a bridge between powerful stakeholders. "In negotiations, you are there because you have to deal with a serious issue. There's no question about that," Albright says. "But you have to connect in some way as a human being and get to know the person."

Albright shared that this experience with Primakov—the late-night rehearsal and silly performance—shifted everything. They got to know each other well, and later on, they'd even share meals at Georgian restaurants where Primakov would introduce Albright to his native cuisine. "We became very good friends."

They would still have tough meetings "where we would criticize each other or each other's countries," she explained, "but in the end, that personal relationship really made a difference."

For Secretary Albright, using levity in the midst of serious issues was an important diplomatic technique. In fact, it was one she had been honing over a decades-long career of navigating delicate and high stakes issues on a global stage.

Earlier in her career, while serving as U.S. ambassador to the United Nations following the first Gulf War, one of Albright's priorities was ensuring that cease-fire sanctions established during the war didn't unravel. She spoke openly about the atrocities committed under Saddam Hussein's rule, making clear that as long as he remained in power, the United States' policy on Iraqi economic sanctions would not change.

Backlash from the region against Albright's position came in many forms, among them poems published in local news outlets comparing her to an "unparalleled serpent." Her response to this vivid depiction? "I happened to have a snake pin and decided to wear it whenever we talked about Iraq." On one such occasion, she was doing a press interview when "all of a sudden the camera zeroes in on me and a journalist asks, 'So why are you wearing that snake pin?'" to which she replied matter-of-factly, "Because Saddam compared me to a serpent."

"I wear pins as a way to add a bit of humor to the day," she told us. "On good days I wore butterflies and balloons and on bad days I wore a lot of carnivorous animals and spiders." When other ambassadors would ask how she was doing on a given day, she'd say, "Read my pins."

Years later, upon discovering that the Russians had bugged the State Department, Secretary Albright wore an enormous bug pin to her meeting with the Russian foreign minister. He knew immediately that the jig was up, prompting a more open, productive conversation.

Albright's pins were lighthearted, but they also conveyed weighty messages and an authority crucial for conducting international diplomacy. Whether through small acts like these or late-night theatrics, Albright consistently used humor to defuse tensions, build personal connections, and lay the groundwork for crucial high-stakes conversations.

Taking Conflict to the Mat

It's no secret that companies need to be nimble to thrive in an increasingly fast-changing world. At a time when experts predict nearly half of S&P 500 companies will be replaced in the index over the next decade (for those bad at math, that's about 250 companies), agility and speed are critical for any leader who wants to win the day.

Such was the case when a potentially contentious and costly copyright dispute arose between the chief executives of Southwest Airlines and a smaller upstart called Stevens Aviation. In the winter of 1992, Southwest Airlines started using the slogan "Just Plane Smart." Unbeknownst to them, though, that slogan was already being used (and under legal claim) by Stevens Aviation, led by CEO Kurt Herwald. Herwald's team encouraged him to take his rival to court.

But taking legal action didn't feel right.

Instead, Herwald opted for a less . . . shall we say, traditional approach to resolving the dispute: He challenged Southwest CEO Herb Kelleher to an arm wrestling match. The winner would get the rights to the slogan, and both would avoid writing sizable checks to their high-priced corporate attorneys.

Kelleher, who in 1968 had set out to create "the world's weirdest airline," was all in. And so the two men prepared to square off in front of forty-five hundred cheering spectators in a packed Dallas stadium in a bizarre and unprecedented event that quickly became known as "the Malice in Dallas."

For Stevens employees, the fun had commenced weeks earlier, when their fearless leader began posting a series of humorous videos to the company intranet documenting his "grueling" training regimen—sweating profusely through curls, deadlifts, and bench presses, all while seemingly lifting an impossible amount of weight.

And now it was showtime. The crowd went wild as the thirty-three-year-old Herwald sprinted into the ring wearing a red silk bathrobe and pumping his fists triumphantly in the air. The cheers only grew louder as Kelleher, nearly thirty years Herwald's senior, made an even grander entrance, bursting into the stadium accompanied by a dozen pom-pom-waving cheerleaders and a colleague dressed as his "trainer" as the theme song from *Rocky* blared through the stadium speakers.

As the clang of a bell echoed through the Texas arena, the crowd roared and the two men interlocked fists in a battle for physical supremacy. Or at least they pretended to for about thirty-five seconds, until Herwald was deemed the undisputed winner.

Upon accepting his victory, Herwald offered to share the slogan with Southwest as a token of respect and good sportsmanship—and a masterstroke of publicity.

Not only did this wacky and utterly unprecedented stunt spare both companies the financial and reputational costs of litigation, it endeared them to their customers and strengthened both their brands—with significant financial results. Southwest was estimated to have earned $6 million from the positive publicity of this event alone. Meanwhile, Stevens experienced 25 percent higher growth than projected over the next four years, during which its revenues rocketed to over $100 million—a trend that Herwald attributes to the name recognition Stevens Aviation received from the match. "[My employees] were so proud of the company and so excited for the visibility that Malice in Dallas gave to their work," he told a reporter. "For months and years after the event, the change to company culture was palpable. Employees felt more connected to one another and to their work."

These two CEOs were nimble enough (in their problem solving, at least; less so in their arm wrestling) to come up with a creative and playful solution that was authentic to them as leaders and to the brands they aspired to create.

Owning the Oops

As a leader (or as someone who aspires to be a leader), it can be tempting to try to appear as though you are always on your game, in the know, cool and under control. But as we've explored, it's often a more powerful move to expose our vulnerability. And it can be a particularly potent approach to not just shine light on, but *make light of* our mistakes. That's because, as leadership expert Dana Bilky Asher puts it, "Laughter serves leaders not in spite of but because of the vulnerability it exposes. It's a straight path from there to trust on a team."

Which is in part why Sara Blakely, founder and CEO of Spanx (who mailed a high heel to the Neiman Marcus buyer), makes a point to showcase her mistakes whenever possible. During regularly held all-company "Oops Meetings," for example, Blakely spotlights a recent mistake she's made, and then (much to the bemusement of new hires who didn't get the memo) she starts to dance. Each time, she chooses a song evocative of her gaffe and invites employees to dance along. Once, when she wanted to highlight the strategic misstep of trying to compete in a product category for longer than she should have, her song choice was "Mr. Roboto," because, as she put it: "It's an amazing song, but it goes on too long."*

From minor slipups to major errors in strategy, Blakely tries to "find the humor in each one, and tell a funny story about it. After the story is told, everybody in the company cheers." Using humor lets her acknowledge mistakes—both her own, and the company's—

---

*The song lasts a full five and a half minutes—331 seconds—while most people can remember exactly four words ("Domo arigato, Mr. Roboto"). Meaning that the song lasts 83 seconds per memorable word.

in a way that doesn't feel heavy. It also encourages people to take big risks of their own. Says Blakely: "I want to free people up inside of the company from fearing failure. Better things happen when you're not paralyzed by fear."

The habit of viewing our mistakes through a comic lens can have a meaningful impact on our psychology. Emerging research at Stanford suggests that people who interpret stories from their lives, both positive and negative, as comedies (as opposed to tragedies or dramas) report feeling less stressed and more energetic, challenged, and fulfilled.

What's more, psychologist Dan McAdams argues that we make active "narrative choices" in the stories we tell ourselves as well as the genre or frame we use for those stories. McAdams is an expert on narrative identity—that is, a person's internalized and evolving life story, which integrates the reconstructed past and imagined future. He posits that by subtly reframing a narrative, we can shift a dramatic or tragic story to one that is more comical or lighthearted, and that making even small story edits can have a big impact on our lives.

In other words, we can usually choose how to frame our failures—*tragic? comic?*—and thereby shift how they impact our lives.

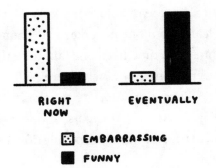

MISTAKES ARE (MOSTLY) OK

RIGHT NOW

EVENTUALLY

☷ EMBARRASSING

■ FUNNY

And beyond being a powerful tool to manage our own psychology, showing that we aren't afraid to laugh about our screw-ups makes others feel safe owning up to theirs.

Just ask Jan, a student of ours who started his career working as a research assistant in the Monterrey Institute of Technology in Mexico. Jan and his team were in the midst of a months-long study focused on understanding the fermentation process in a certain type of algae. After running an expensive test of their process in a large bioreactor, the research assistants realized that the sample had been contaminated—and the entire experiment ruined.

Given that the majority of contaminations result from human error, the team knew the mistake had likely been their fault. Nervous and disappointed, they approached the doctor who was supervising their research to break the bad news.

After listening to Jan's explanation and sensing the nervousness in his team, the doctor paused briefly. Then, with a playful smile, he asked: "Was it Pinky?"

The team was perplexed. "Who's Pinky?"

"Pinky is this pesky bacteria that's been doing rounds in the lab," the doctor explained. "He pops up in a sample every once in a while just to keep us on our toes."

"At that point," Jan recalls, "the team just laughed. It dissolved our fears. And then pretty quickly, we got to brainstorming how to solve the problem."

Using humor in the face of failure can help us manage our emotions so we can learn from our mistakes and bounce back quickly, decreasing the transition time from one failure to the next attempt. As leadership expert Dana Bilky Asher writes: "We cannot lead if we cannot learn. And yet, our capacity to take in and process new information—to generate new insights and true growth—shuts down in response to the fear of letting people down. Laughter opens us up again."

In Pursuit of Purpose

It was the Spring of 2015, and Daryn Dodson, a board member of the ice cream manufacturer Ben and Jerry's, was working with the company's leadership to prepare for the UN Climate Summit in Paris later that year. As the largest meeting of climate negotiators in the world (with more than 190 nations to attend), many hoped the summit would produce a groundbreaking, legally binding agreement to keep global warming in check.

You might be wondering: what does climate change have to do with an ice cream company?

Since its founding, a core part of Ben and Jerry's business and operating model has centered around the company's commitment to helping solve the world's most pressing social and environmental problems. In fact, when the company was acquired by Unilever in 2000, an unconventional term of the deal was the creation of an independent Ben & Jerry's board of directors to maintain focus on these issues.

Which brings us back to Daryn Dodson, a member of the board. After careful consideration, Dodson, the rest of the board, and the management team defined their strategy and got to work.

They released a new ice cream flavor, "Save Our Swirled," and an accompanying video called "If it's melted, it's ruined," together aimed at building awareness of the climate crisis and encouraging fans in more than 35 nations to sign a petition calling on world leaders to keep global temperature rise under 2 degrees Celsius. As you might expect, the video wasn't all serious. It showed a globby mess of ice cream melting in reverse—that is, refreezing into a deliciously frozen product as the narrator outlined the importance of acting now to reverse the trend of global warming. Or as they put it: why ice caps, like ice cream, are best kept frozen.

As Dodson reflected, "At Ben and Jerry's, we have a very serious side when we're supporting activists in their respective communities, and we stand up for our values. But we also are very aware that movements need humor—and that humorous content sometimes goes viral in ways that can better support these movements." Their approach worked, as the video was widely shared and garnered thousands of signatures to the petition. By using a lighthearted approach while sharing the gravity of the situation, Dodson explained, "we were able to offer a small bit of levity to a really challenging problem in a way that made it accessible to many people who may not have the time or energy to understand."

Climate change is just one of the movements you'll find on the "Issues We Care About" section of Ben and Jerry's website, which also includes LGBT equality, criminal justice reform, and democracy. In more than forty years since the company's founding, Ben and Jerry's may be as well known for its activism as for its delicious pints of Half Baked. And over that time, the Ben and Jerry's team and board have consistently tackled a multitude of gravely serious issues with levity.

For example, a few years later, in 2017, when Australia's Parliament had not yet legalized same-sex marriage, the company instituted a country-wide ban on "same-scoop servings" and installed rainbow-topped postal boxes in each of its Australian shops, making it easier for customers to contact their local parliamentary representatives. As journalist Jelisa Castrodale of *Vice* reported at the time, "even though their approach might seem silly or trivial, it has added fuel to a dialogue that's been stagnating and has reminded Australians that this inequality is still unresolved." The goal of the ban, as Dodson shared, was not just to regain momentum among those who were already in support, but also to "connect the movement to our fans that may not agree."

The examples go on: a partnership with the Advancement Project to create a new ice cream flavor called *Justice ReMix'd*, which the official 2019 release described as a cinnamon and chocolate ice cream with chunks of cinnamon bun dough and an aftertaste of "ending structural racism in our broken criminal legal system"; a protest at the White House in support of Democracy Awakening that ended in Ben Cohen and Jerry Greenfield being arrested while eating ice cream in handcuffs. A photo of the arrest spread like wildfire, but not without purpose: As Dodson explained, "Many fans that may not have been aware of the principles of the movement—around immigrants' rights, or around the people that couldn't exercise their constitutional right to vote in North Carolina due to various voter ID laws—were inspired to read more and take action to support communities that had been disenfranchised by being refused their right to vote."

The movements that Dodson has devoted his life and work to tackling—at Ben and Jerry's and beyond—are serious, systemic, and pressing. And Dodson was clear that in this context, humor is like salt: you don't want to use it all the time, and a little goes a long way.

Still, said Dodson, "I think humor is a wonderful way to express the careful walk along the tightrope of the difficult, underlying issues of a culture, or in pursuit of an incredibly audacious mission. To relax ourselves as we pursue our purposes—or porpoises, for the fishermen out there—and make a difference in society."

Pedestals Are Out

When it comes to contemporary attitudes about leadership, another big piece of the puzzle is *hierarchy:* How do leaders cultivate an environment where they can simultaneously project authority and approachability? During his tenure as CEO of Twitter, Dick Costolo masterfully applied levity to connect with his teams and dispel unhelpful tension caused by hierarchy and status.

"I remember being in the elevator one Monday morning when all the new hires were starting," Costolo recalls. "One person in the elevator says in this hushed whisper 'That's the CEO!' And I laugh and go 'I'm right here! Hello! I'm not a hologram, I can hear you! My name's Dick. Nice to meet you!' Everyone chuckled, and it immediately changed the power dynamic." For a few moments, at least, the act of laughing together evaporated the hierarchy and made him seem less intimidating and more approachable. Costolo began doing this regularly, using his daily elevator rides as an opportunity to connect with employees and even joke about his status as something of a celebrity figure within the company. The effect rippled far beyond each individual ride as stories of these encounters spread among employees.

At one point in the American workplace, such an interaction between a CEO and the rank and file would have been unthinkable. But today, pedestals are out and approachability is in. According to a 2018 Gallup report on U.S. workplace engagement, an approachable manager can increase employee engagement by more than 30 percent. Moreover, employees who felt they could open up and talk to their manager about non-work-related issues were seven times more engaged than those who felt non-work conversations were off limits.

Perhaps the easiest and most effective way for leaders to humanize themselves to their team is a healthy dose of self-deprecation. In one study, researchers Colette Hoption, Julian Barling, and Nick Turner sought to understand the effects of humor on status differences between leaders and followers. They found that leaders who use self-deprecating humor are subsequently rated higher on measures of both trustworthiness and leadership ability by their employees.

HOW TO BE APPROACHABLE

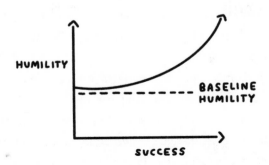

Warren Buffett is a classic example of a leader whose sincere style of self-deprecating humor—what Forbes has called "his under-appreciated superpower"—projects a "guy next door" kind of humility, despite his having a net worth that rivals the GDP of several small countries.

At his famed annual meetings, Buffett has been known to garner laughs at his own expense, thanks to his folksy jabs poking fun at everything from his age (when asked how he wanted to be remembered at his funeral, he replied, "I want them to all be saying 'That's the oldest-looking corpse I ever saw'") to his eating habits ("In thirty years, one-quarter of the calories I've consumed have come from Coca-Cola. That's not an exaggeration. I'm one-quarter Coca-Cola. I'm not sure which quarter") to his regrettable business decisions ("Today, I would rather prep for a colonoscopy than issue Berkshire shares").

For Dick Costolo, being self-effacing isn't just a way to earn likability points—it's also critical to his success as a leader. As he explained: "My job as a leader isn't to prevent mistakes from happening; my job as a leader is to correct them as quickly as possible when they do happen. However, if nobody feels comfortable bringing me the bad news—it's going to take me a lot longer to correct those mistakes."

Leaning Tower of Gratitude

A student of ours recalled a former manager she'd worked with, Scott, who used levity to signal gratitude in a way that has stuck with her to this day.

Scott had been her project manager on a content writing team for an up-and-coming biotech company in California. About halfway into a yearlong project, Scott's life got a little busy—not only was he slammed at work with other projects, he and his wife had just welcomed their first baby. The more he was called away from his team, the more he could feel himself struggling to show up for them in the way they needed.

So he came up with a creative way to show them he appreciated their work. One night, Scott stayed late, temporarily eschewing deadlines and paternal duties to fish hundreds of empty LaCroix cans out of recycling bins all over campus. The next morning, Scott's team walked into the office and were greeted by an unusual sight: Everyone's desks were arranged in the middle of the room, with a giant LaCroix-can pyramid atop them reaching close to the ceiling. On top of the pyramid was a little flag that read, "I see you all reaching for great heights."

The structure may not have been a work of architectural art, but symbolically it was brilliant—a lighthearted way to show that he saw and appreciated the hard work his team had been doing.

"It sounds trite and kind of random," our former student recalled. "But from a morale perspective, we did need to feel like us working our asses off was being noticed. There was something about him slaving over this elaborate and ridiculous display of appreciation that made us all go 'ok cool, he gets it. He's in this with us.'"

Recognition of hard work matters, especially when it comes to retaining talent. A decades-long study of two hundred thousand managers and employees conducted by OC Tanner found that 79 percent of people who leave their jobs cite "lack of appreciation" as a primary reason.

We all want to have our wins celebrated, but when the acknowledgment feels insincere, our bullshit radar goes off. Unexpected, playful moments of praise or recognition can often be more meaningful than "official" ones because they signal that someone is not only paying attention to what we're doing well, but cares enough to go out of their way to celebrate it.

Put another way: No one stays up all night constructing a tower of recyclable trash unless they mean it.

Balancing Gravity and Levity

It was November 2000, and the notoriously colorful magnate, philanthropist, author, and Virgin Group founder Richard Branson was launching Virgin Mobile in Australia with his team. His new CMO, Jean Oelwang, had recently come over from a much stodgier operation where joking around was not only frowned upon, but viewed as detrimental to the bottom line. And now she found herself standing above Sydney Harbor, gazing toward the sky where her new boss was hanging upside-down from a bungee cord connected to a speeding helicopter. The plan was for him to float down and land on the harbor, where he would "free" dozens of customers waiting trapped inside large steel cages—cages that represented the metaphorical bondage of their existing cellular plans.

It was a wild stunt—the kind Branson is legendary for—but he still wanted to find a way to welcome his new CMO and establish the tone of their working relationship to come. So when the death-defying helicopter escapade came to an end, Branson approached Oelwang, who had his prepared remarks waiting. When she handed him the speech, Branson squinted at the first page for ten seconds—befuddled and visibly vexed—before flipping to the second and third. Something was wrong, thought Oelwang and the rest of the team. Then he cut the silence: "I'm dyslexic . . . you put the lines too close together. I can't do the speech!"

The air left the room.

Then a mischievous grin sprang across Branson's goateed face, and he began to laugh. Oelwang and her new colleagues realized he was joking, and they burst out laughing as well.

Any intimidation Oelwang might have felt was defused instantly. In the twenty-plus years they have worked together since that memorable first day, Oelwang says she's come to appreciate how "joy and humor speed up the process to trust and respect. They create a safe space to grow a relationship." In fact, she believes that "from that moment Richard played the prank on me right before the launch of Virgin Mobile, it set the scene for the rest of our partnership over the last twenty years."*

Oelwang turned out to be the perfect yin to Branson's yang. Together, her more serious nature and his penchant for mischief made for powerful alchemy, allowing them to forge a beautiful partnership filled with levity and laughter, "without losing sight of the importance of the work we're doing or sacrificing the quality of delivery."

Four years following the helicopter stunt in Sydney Harbor, Branson was hosting a series of meetings at his home on Necker Island in the Caribbean to form the Elders, a group founded by Nelson Mandela to work together for global peace and human rights.

---

*A little different from the scene her last manager had set on Jean's first day at the firm, when he had given her two books: Sun Tzu's *Art of War* and Irma Rombauer's recipe bible *The Joy of Cooking*. As Oelwang recalled, the message was harrowingly clear: Learn to go to war and crush competitors, or quit the rat race and cook your way to domestic bliss. Sigh.

The inaugural brainstorming sessions included Archbishop Desmond Tutu, President Jimmy Carter, retired secretary-general of the United Nations Kofi Annan, the musician and activist Peter Gabriel, and other world leaders.

Leading up to the event, Oelwang and her team had spent months planning every detail of the meetings. They had prepared elaborate daily schedules and compiled hundreds of pages of heavily researched presentations, which detailed the pressing human rights issues this group was convening to discuss.

Branson, however, had other ideas.

As Oelwang describes, the night before the Elders arrived, "we all convened to go over the plan for the retreat. Richard and Peter Gabriel took one look at our materials and put our PowerPoints in the trash bin. Richard and Peter said that they wanted to make sure that this [event] was more human. Richard insisted that we change the whole agenda to make half the day play and half the day work."

The idea bordered on ludicrous—world leaders were flying in from across the globe and dedicating multiple days to furthering the mission of peace and human rights, and Branson wanted them to spend *half* of their time together *playing?* Oelwang recalls pushing back, saying, "We have to have the whole day focused on content. People are coming all the way here—they're going to expect that."

But Branson prevailed. The team reworked the weekend agenda according to his half work / half play ratio. In addition to the structured sessions, the convening was punctuated by playful activities— like Gabriel and Branson teaching Archbishop Tutu to swim.

And as it turned out, the afternoons of play were where the real work happened. Most notably, it was during one of those afternoons, as President Carter and Archbishop Tutu sat together on the beach, their feet in the sand, that the two men created what would eventually become the founding values for the Elders. It was in this beautiful moment, when the alchemy of levity, connection, and joy combined with the gravity of the work being done to yield profound results. Oelwang had created the rigorous foundation necessary for the group to immerse themselves in the issues at hand, and Branson had given his peers the room they needed to think, dream, and create.

Branson holds steadfast in his belief that serious moments—like this once-in-a-lifetime meeting with some of the greatest leaders of a generation to discuss some of the most intractable global problems of our times—are actually the ones in which levity is needed most. In this case, the illustrious and diverse group of world leaders not only had fun together, forging a lasting partnership replete with mischief and revelry, they also did a whole lot of good for humanity. Amen.

And as Branson and Oelwang remind us, the balance between gravity and levity is not just a powerful strategy for tackling serious issues, it's also a potent recipe for a winning team.

* * *

Each of these stories features different leaders, from different fields, in different parts of the world, but they share a common narrative: A highly respected leader, with an estimable track record of success (and perhaps the ego to go with it), injects levity into a situation dripping with seriousness, with very positive results.

The academic data back up these anecdotes: Humor works, even in (especially in) the most dramatic circumstances.

So what to do? Let's close this chapter with a little exercise. If you were Leslie Blodgett and had to write a full-page ad in *The New York Times* to help your flagging business, what would you write? If you were Secretary of State Madeleine Albright and had to sing a duet with your biggest adversary, what would you sing? (Don't forget they have nukes.) What would be your LaCroix can pyramid? Your get-Carter-and-Tutu-to-dig-their-toes-in-the-sand moment?

Humor is a superpower, but unlike invisibility, laser vision, and being superhuman, it's one we all secretly possess.*

---

*But don't expect a Marvel movie contract. Unless you get big and green when you're angry. Then, maybe.

CHAPTER 6

Creating a

Culture of Levity

"I'm struck by how laughter connects you with people. It's almost impossible to maintain any kind of distance or any sense of social hierarchy when you're just howling with laughter."

—John Cleese

Toy Story **was** one of the most creatively ambitious, lucrative, and trailblazing films of a generation. The world's first feature length computer-animated film, it was a quaint tale about the adventures of a ragtag band of lovable toys who come alive when humans are out of sight.

In many ways, the making of the movie mirrored the plot itself. The small, impassioned creative team would routinely pull all-nighters during which the eclectic bunch of engineers and animators at Pixar would—not unlike Woody and Buzz—come alive.

Pixar's culture was imbued with an infectious, energizing spirit of levity and play. Some nights, that meant mini-golf tournaments and scooter races in the cramped hallways of their Los Angeles studio. (These recurring contests were so competitive that senior producer Tom Porter was once awoken at home in the middle of the night to return to the studio and protect his long-held record.) The interns held elaborate dress-down Fridays, showing up in matching costumes like Jedis or Cub Scouts. The company hosted "Pixarpalooza," with as many as twenty different bands of Pixar employees playing covers of their favorite songs.

But these traditions didn't come at the cost of productivity. In fact, many regard Pixar's teams as some of the most hardworking and productive in the industry.

This was no happy accident. Ed Catmull, the former president of

Pixar and Walt Disney Animation Studios, believed that levity and play were foundational to building productive, creative teams. This is a theory validated by research: In a study of 352 employees across 54 teams, researchers Nale Lehmann-Willenbrock and Joseph Allen videotaped hourlong team meetings and then analyzed supervisors' ratings of team performance. The teams that had humor demonstrated more functional communication and problem-solving behaviors, and performed better as a team, both during the meeting itself and over time. It was exactly this kind of playful culture that allowed the teams at Pixar to thrive.

Under Catmull's leadership, Pixar launched blockbusters like *A Bug's Life, Monsters, Inc.,* and *Finding Nemo* and developed the cutting-edge computer technology that revolutionized animated film (and made grown adults weep over bugs, fish, and fuzzy blue monsters in the process). In Catmull's view, that success was due in large part to the camaraderie and resilience among workers at Pixar, which was itself a product of the laughter-filled culture they'd cultivated. As Catmull reflected, "Lots of humor and levity in the good times solidify the relationships, making it easier for people to call on one another during the hard times."

In short, it came down to culture.

It seems obvious that a culture in which employees can do their best work while having fun is desirable. So why do so many workplaces feel like they're straight out of *Office Space*?*

If yours is one of them, this chapter is for you. In the pages that follow, we'll offer stories, frameworks, and tips that will help you cultivate a culture of humor and levity at your organization.

But before diving in, we want to stress that the application of these techniques isn't universal. You might be comfortable in the

---

* A reference to Mike Judge's paean to white-collar drudgery. If you haven't seen this . . . yeah, we're gonna need you to go ahead and watch it ASAP. If you could do that, that would be *greeeat*. Which is a reference you'll understand only after you watch it.

spotlight, pulling your company's culture toward you, or instead prefer to influence culture more indirectly by elevating a charismatic co-worker or altering your office's physical space. Like eating a Reese's, there's no one way to build culture.

Your mission, should you choose to accept it, is to refract each principle and tactic through your authentic leadership style and your unique organization—then adopt the ones that are most resonant. In the process, you'll foster stronger relationships and empower your teams to do their best work, all while creating the kind of environment where people *want* to work.

Set the Tone from the Top

Unsurprisingly, leaders have a disproportionate influence on organizational culture. One of the most effective ways we've seen leaders engender a culture of levity is by publicly embodying—and enabling—humor, sending strong, consistent signals that levity and play are desired and embraced.

SHOWCASE YOUR FUNNY

We've explored many stories of leaders showcasing their humor: how Leslie Blodgett's ad in *The New York Times* got employees buzzing; how Stephen Curry's spirited impression of Steve Ballmer relaxed his team of partners and allowed them to feel more comfortable; how Richard Branson's daring helicopter stunt matched his cheeky prank when he landed, reinforcing that play was valued and encouraged at Virgin. What these stories—and the ones you are about to read—have in common is that they allow leaders to signal that they aren't the type to take themselves too seriously. These public displays of levity set the tone for the culture and give tacit permission for others in the organization to follow their lead.

Spontaneous humor is a common tool used by those CEOs who

are most effective at setting a tone of levity. Why is it so effective? Surprise! (No, there's no actual surprise. The answer is "surprise.") When humor feels planned, you lose the crucial element of surprise. In this way, a punch line should come like a punch. If your audience is braced for impact, it's harder to knock them out. (And they're uncomfortable waiting for you to deliver it.) No wonder one of the first pieces of advice most comedians give to noncomedians is never to start a story with "I have a funny story. . . ." When people perceive that you're trying to be funny, all of a sudden you have something to prove.

Organic humor has a far lower bar. When you are simply reacting to the moment (the "here and now" from trusty chapter 3), anything even *slightly* surprising or unserious—the smallest gesture of play—can elicit laughter. In short: If it feels planned, it better be good. If you're onstage and accidentally drop a peanut, it's comedic gold.

It's easy for us to say "Go be spontaneously funny!" but doing so in practice is far more difficult. That's why we suggest focusing on creating favorable conditions for spontaneous humor that doesn't feel forced. And the simplest way to do that is to showcase where it already exists—your most naturally playful, fun work relationships.

Dick Costolo was no stranger to this strategy; while at Twitter, he had a number of employees he'd call on to fill this role. Among them was April Underwood, a longtime colleague and senior product director whom Costolo would periodically invite onstage for companywide presentations.

The two knew each other well from working together at Google, and their playful, preexisting rapport helped Costolo come across as a real person—with a real sense of humor. By inviting Underwood onstage, Costolo was tacitly establishing her as every other employee's proxy; seeing her play and rib the boss allowed them to vicariously do the same. As Underwood reflected, "There's no substitute for that moment when something unexpected happens and the people onstage respond to it with humor. The fact that it's unplanned, unfolding in the moment, makes it even funnier. And it was a safe way to do it, because we could play off each other in a way that was completely natural—and fun."

A similar dynamic is at play in those *SNL* sketches in which actors "break" character and laugh at their own hilarity. It works because we can see the actors as humans in a moment that they're experiencing along with us—which can sometimes be even funnier than the sketch they planned. The actor is no longer ahead of the audience. By giving up control to Underwood and reacting in real time, Costolo lets everyone else be in the moment with him.

This is a technique that Google's founders, Larry Page and Sergey Brin—along with Eric Schmidt, when he later joined as CEO—used from the start.

Not long after Google's founding, Page and Brin instituted an hourlong companywide meeting at the end of each week called TGIF (Thank Goodness It's Friday).* For the first thirty minutes, the team reviewed news and product launches from the past week, provided demos for unreleased products, and celebrated recent wins. The final thirty minutes consisted of a question-and-answer session during which any Google employee could query† the leadership team about anything they wanted.

Googlers enjoyed both the subject matter and the style in which the meetings were held. They loved the fact that no topic was off the table, from cellphone features to election results. But the witty repartee between Page and Brin (and later Schmidt as well) was often the real highlight, especially when Brin's farcical sense of humor was on full display.

---

* Search "Google TGIF 1999 video" on YouTube for a treat. And Google "TGIF $14.99 Menu" to treat yourself to two grill favorites plus mashed potatoes and lemon butter broccoli for an affordable price.

† Yes, that was a subtle search engine pun. Please feel free to boo(lean).

TGIF at Google frequently resembled a comedy show. Schmidt recalled that "the humor came out completely naturally" when the two of them were onstage together; they were able to play off each other, showcasing the lighthearted banter they enjoyed behind closed doors.

The leaders' goal was clear and purposeful: to inspire a relaxed form of leadership. As Schmidt reflected, "You get the leadership you inspire. If the leadership of the company is relaxed and humorous and having fun, the other people will have permission, within the appropriate boundaries, to do the same thing."

They set a cultural tone that has remained consistent for over twenty years: Google is a company where people were empowered to have fun and be themselves.

Of course, not all leaders are comfortable putting their own sense of humor on display.* But there are plenty of ways to cultivate a culture of levity and signal that humor is valued in your organization without putting yourself in the spotlight.

PLAY ALONG

One of the first rules of improv comedy is the concept of "Yes, and"—the rule that when your scene partner makes an offer (either explicitly or implied), you always agree with the premise and add something new to it. In *Bossypants*, Tina Fey explains:

> If I start a scene with "I can't believe it's so hot in here," and you just say, "Yeah . . . ," we're kind of at a standstill.

> But if I say, "I can't believe it's so hot in here," and you say, "What did you expect? We're in hell." Or if I say, "I can't believe it's so hot in here," and you say, "Yes, this can't be good for the wax figures." Or if I say, "I can't believe it's so

---

*That said, if you've got it—flaunt it, sister (sassy snap).

hot in here," and you say, "I told you we shouldn't have crawled into this dog's mouth," now we're getting somewhere.

The "Yes, and" approach adds to the scene, helps the humor develop, and establishes trust between scene partners.

The surest path to encouraging a culture of levity is to "Yes, and" the levity that arises naturally from co-workers and teams, argues Kelly Leonard, author of—wait for it—*Yes, And.*

Nowhere is this more important (or acutely felt) than when grassroots acts of levity come at your own expense. As the CEO of Rover, a popular platform that matches pet owners with experienced dog walkers and pet sitters in their area, Aaron Easterly says he routinely encourages his employees to make their own fun, even if it involves making fun of him.

Case in point: On the morning of the company's eighth anniversary, Easterly's team decided to honor the occasion with doughnuts and a homespun party game entitled Two Truths and a Lie: The How Well Do You Know Aaron Easterly Contest. The quiz was just ten questions, each consisting of three facts about Easterly. As you've likely inferred (you are a smart bunch), two were true and one was a lie; the challenge was to guess the lie.

Some (embarrassing) truths the game revealed about Easterly:

- He once purchased a stick shift Jeep, forgetting momentarily that he didn't know how to drive a stick shift.
- He showed up to a board of directors dinner and was unable to eat it because he'd filled up on Fudge Stripes on the walk over.
- He once mistakenly referred to a roomful of MSN executives as being from AOL multiple times during a pitch.

"And so all the dumb things that I've done for a twenty-year span were immortalized," Easterly recalls. Instead of worrying about his most embarrassing screw-ups being meticulously documented for his colleagues' amusement, he joined in on the fun, played along, and elaborated on the stories at his employees' eager requests.

Former Google chairman Eric Schmidt also knows a thing or two about not getting in the way of humor at his expense. Back when he was the head of product development at Sun Microsystems, Schmidt arrived at work one day to find a Volkswagen Beetle in the middle of his office. It seemed that several next-level pranksters had purchased the vehicle, taken it apart, carted it into his office overnight, and reassembled it before he arrived in the morning.* Schmidt knew that his reaction to this elaborate trick (and act of mechanical wizardry) was quite important. He recalled, "I said to myself, 'Oh well. My schedule has changed and now it's time to play along.'"

Instead of pulling away, he leaned (or more accurately, *walked*) into his team's humor, conducting meetings inside the Beetle for the next few days.

PLAY ALONG

---

*Incidentally, April Fools' Day was a sacred holiday at Sun. They do not mess around. One year, employees transported the entire contents of the CEO's office into a shipping container in the company parking lot. Another time, an executive's desk was found at the bottom of a tank at the San Francisco Aquarium.

Embrace the Underground

At Pixar, Ed Catmull saw the zany rituals that filled the halls with laughter, delight, and cute furry monsters as the true connective tissue of the company. But he's never believed that it's a leader's job to try to dictate the terms of culture from on high. As he says: "Fun is not a top-down thing."

On the contrary, a culture of levity can—and must—come from all levels. And if you look, you'll find potential energy all around. In our interviews, we found that the sources of this potential—the employees who can help create this culture—were commonly described as one of three archetypes: **Instigators, Culture Carriers,** and **Hidden Gems**.

Culture Carriers are natural leaders and rising stars in the organization, for whom humor also happens to be a natural strength. **Hidden Gems** are diligent, under-the-radar high performers, who provide unexpected opportunities for levity. And **Instigators** are rabble-rousers* and rule breakers who do things differently and tend to be nonconformist by nature.

How to leverage each archetype—and the degree of their impact on your organization—depends on your current culture and goals. Throw an Instigator into Pixar, and she may fit right in. Throw an Instigator into the Yankees clubhouse, though, and he may shake things up. Or, rather, he *did* shake things up.

Instigators

There are few workplaces with higher stakes or higher pressure than Major League Baseball. And yet, as New York Yankees legend

---

* Not to be confused with *Rebel Rousers,* the 1970 American independent outlaw biker film starring Jack Nicholson. Or with rabbit rousers, the people who go around to farms playing bugles by the rabbit warren to let the rabbits know the day has begun.

Alex Rodriguez tells it, a culture of levity was a key driver of the Yankees' 2009 World Series title. But just a few years earlier, the culture couldn't have been more different.

Even if you don't know a bunt from a balk,* you have heard of the New York Yankees—the most storied team in baseball. But with so much history and tradition comes a certain aversion to rocking the boat. Longtime Yankees owner George Steinbrenner, who ran the team for thirty-seven years, even famously instituted a strict policy on hair: nothing long in the back, and no facial hair other than mustaches. "We were the Goldman Sachs of baseball," Rodriguez joked.

But when the team gathered for spring training in 2006, there was a lot of buzz—and not all of it good—around one of the team's new additions: center fielder Johnny Damon, who had been acquired from the rival Red Sox in the offseason.

Damon was colorful, to say the least. He reveled in attention. He drove a black Ferrari. He titled his autobiography *Idiot*. He once dropped a pumpkin off his thirty-fourth-floor balcony for kicks. How would a guy like this—a textbook Instigator—fit into the formal culture of the Yankees clubhouse?

He didn't. And that's why it worked. On day one, says Rodriguez, Damon walked into the clubhouse "at six in the morning, with his boom box playing Kid Rock really, really loud" (to be fair, it would feel deeply inappropriate to play Kid Rock quietly). "It was a *moment*," Rodriguez recalled.

Rather than making unwanted waves, the lighthearted energy Damon brought to the team electrified the group. "It unlocked a lot of people's sense of humor," Rodriguez said. Not only that, "it made us play better. It made us relax and our performance improved." It wasn't long before other players were getting in on the fun. Pitcher

---

*Naomi was a collegiate athlete and Jennifer works out in flip-flops. We'll let you guess who wrote this sentence.

AJ Burnett started a new tradition: Every time a teammate hit a home run or had a walk-off hit to end a game, Burnett would be waiting to smash them in the face with a pie.

Damon's energy was infectious, and Rodriguez recognized early how it helped the Yankees thrive: "In a world of sabermetrics where everyone is being appraised by numbers—home runs, RBI, slugging percentages—there are people who walk into the clubhouse and are game changers. People who shift the ambiance, the energy. It makes the clubhouse lighter and as a result, the team plays better."

Damon, and Instigators like him, challenge the culture head-on. While their approaches tend to be riskier and more disruptive, they can also prompt cultural step changes—but only if leaders, like Rodriguez, are perceptive and flexible enough to embrace them and recognize their impact.

When Pixar's culture hit a bump in the road, it was the Instigators who spearheaded the turnaround. As Catmull reflected, years after the company's founding, the early employees (once known for being a young and rowdy group) had moved into a different phase of life. Many had started families and were raising young children, so instead of staying late after work to have fun together and decompress (read: launch rockets made from five-gallon water cooler jugs* in the parking lot, once shattering a car windshield), they'd leave early to be with their families. As a new crop of youngsters joined the company, they took their social cues from the more staid culture that had taken root. As Catmull describes, he woke up one day and realized: "We've lost our fun."

Catmull's response was to call on his Instigators, surface his observations, and encourage them to take larger cultural swings. According to Catmull, all it took was this nudge of encouragement and the Instigators kicked into gear, rallying the troops, breaking rules, and reigniting the fun. After one such nudging, the Animation De-

---

*Now, this is meaningful water cooler conversation.

partment decided to dismantle an old truck. Then over the weekend, without asking for permission, they reassembled the truck in the middle of the Animation Area. While a truck in the studio might seem inconvenient to some, as Catmull puts it simply, "These are great signals."

When the culture strays off course, Instigators are catalysts—lightning bolts of fun who reignite the subversion and playfulness. Says Catmull: "There will always be people in the company who are a little 'out there.' If everyone were like them, people probably wouldn't get much done. But the culture needs some of these people, because they signal to everyone else that it's okay to be different."

Identifying and elevating these Instigators encourages fun and play and signals that it's okay to break rules, break windshields, and blast Kid Rock every once in a while.

Culture Carriers

Culture Carriers are your rising stars who are widely respected throughout the organization and also happen to have an affinity for humor and play. If supported and elevated, they can be a secret weapon in cultivating an enduring, contagious culture of levity.

To illustrate their role, let's travel back to 2015 and drop by the fast-growing online education startup Coursera. CEO (and former president of Yale University) Rick Levin was beginning his weekly all-hands meeting as usual, running through a list of current priorities and progress achieved. But this particular meeting featured an uninvited guest. The mystery man peered eerily through his Google Glass headset from behind Levin as he began heckling the distinguished CEO while employees looked on, mesmerized and delighted.

The man *appeared* to be Sebastian Thrun, CEO of Coursera's top competitor, Udacity. As the meeting went on, his taunts became more and more aggressive. With the demeanor of an unhinged supervillain, he routinely interrupted Levin's remarks to lambaste his rival CEO, as well as Coursera itself in an absurdly dramatized German accent: "Oooo . . . you think you ist so fancy und smart, yah? My self-driving cars vud drive circles around you!" he cackled.

These comedic diatribes were met with uproarious laughter and applause as Coursera's employees relished the over-the-top haranguing. Yet Levin remained unfazed.

"Thrun" was in fact Connor Diemand-Yauman, one of Coursera's earliest hires and by all accounts a star employee. Widely respected for his strong work ethic and rapid rise in the company, Diemand-Yauman was also infamous among colleagues for his mischievous sense of humor and his ability to breathe life into dry, mundane moments.

Months earlier, Diemand-Yauman had arrived at the company Halloween party in the very same Sebastian Thrun costume. Levin could simply have laughed along with the rest of his team at Diemand-Yauman's antics—but instead, he leaned in, using his position to showcase and amplify Diemand-Yauman's gesture by asking if he'd like to take "Thrun" more public.

By not only taking the shenanigans in stride but actively championing them, Levin consistently endorsed Diemand-Yauman and his approach to levity, giving room for others to do the same: "Rick and the other senior leaders stressed our agency in sculpting Coursera into the organization we aspired to work in," said Diemand-Yauman. "They gave us so much room to play, create joy, and find new ways to enhance the culture (and ultimately, our company's performance)."

Levin's recognition of Coursera's culture carriers was brilliant, reverberating, and profound. The result of their dynamic was a lasting culture of quirk and play at Coursera, which, years after Diemand-Yauman's departure, is still cited by employees as a primary driver for their coming to (and staying in) the organization.

To activate Culture Carriers, welcome them into the fray, sharing challenges and opportunities that they can help address from the bottom up. Treat them like peers, share organizational concerns, and allow them to solve key problems with you—adding their own flavor of play. You'll be cultivating the growth of someone who can provide major value, both now and in the future.

Hidden Gems

Our third archetype can be easy to miss. Hidden Gems are the high-performing, hardworking individuals who often fly under the radar with inspiring (and inspired) skills, quirks, and hobbies.

Let's revisit Hiroki Asai—the former head of Apple's Creative Design Studio who loved putting his creativity to work on company-wide All Hands meetings. Prior to one particular All Hands meeting, Asai had learned that one of the more junior team members, a skilled and dedicated designer, was also a classically trained singer—a fact that few of her colleagues knew.

As Asai took the stage that day, he invited the employee to join him, explaining to the crowd that she was there to share a recent win from her team. But as soon as she took the mic, the curtains of the enormous stage swung open to reveal a hidden gospel choir, who immediately broke into song, backing up the exceptionally talented employee who had begun belting onstage.

The room erupted in delight as more performers, who had been secretly planted among the audience, danced their way toward the stage. The auditorium was filled with cheers of appreciation, laughter, and harmony (both musical and interpersonal) as the singer brought the house down in front of her two thousand colleagues.

While you might not think a flash mob gospel choir screams (or sings) "good for business," Asai would disagree.

First, spotlighting the unique talents of Hidden Gems—these diligent, often overlooked high performers who live in all corners of your organization—is a potent recipe for humor, and the joy that comes with it. It comes back to an ingredient we know and love: the inherent *surprise* of revealing their talents creates a moment of delight. It doesn't need to be funny, it just needs to be true to prompt laughter and joy.

Far beyond this moment of shared laughter, it helps to shape the culture in a more profound and lasting way. As Asai saw it, by elevating the Hidden Gems in his organization (the "quiet heroes," as he called them), he was signaling that every person in the organization—regardless of tenure or status—was valued not just for what they produced at work, but for what they loved to do outside work. It signaled that whatever your unique passions and personality are, they are welcome here. Hidden Gems are some of your most powerful allies in sending this message.

And the relationship goes the other way as well: When people feel comfortable bringing their whole selves to work—personal passions, quirks, things that make them unique and special—their senses of humor will come as well.

Institutionalize Levity

So you've said some witty things publicly (or at least signaled your sense of humor has a heartbeat) and found some killer Instigators / Culture Carriers / Hidden Gems who you're hellbent on unlocking. But you're not satisfied with that—you want to create a culture of levity that stands the test of time!

This brings us to the art of *institutionalizing* levity, building it into the fabric of your organization itself.

CURATE DEFINING MOMENTS

Pause for a moment and consider: What have been the most defining moments of your current job? When you think about what has been most memorable and important—that had the most impact on how you feel about your job—which moments come to mind?

Our brains are wired in such a way that we remember our lives less like a film strip of the experience unfolding than like a series of snapshots. And these snapshots—those that flooded your mind when you paused to reflect—are not captured at random.

Instead, they disproportionately come in two flavors: the most *emotionally heightened* moment of an experience (the "peak"), and the *final* moment of an experience (the "end"). This is driven by a heuristic that Daniel Kahneman and Barbara Fredrickson refer to as the Peak-End Rule.

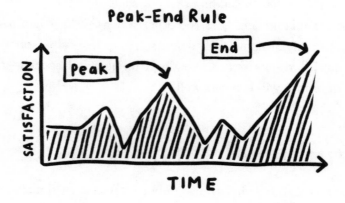

Consequently, these two types of moments weigh heavily in how we remember the events, experiences, jobs, and even people in our lives. Understanding this phenomenon gives us a window into how we can shape the shared memories of our culture and the emotions that reverberate within our employees long after any experience has passed.

Crafting your culture, Asai says, is similar to creating a family picture wall at home. "When you do that, you take very deliberate steps to celebrate people, moments, and places you've gone, you frame those moments and you hang them on the wall." Those moments, he says, become a constant reminder of the family's values—or in the case of an organization, the values and culture of the organization.

When convening everyone in an organization, every moment counts—which is exactly why Asai invested so much in bringing people together in unusual and levity-infused ways. From a gospel choir to a video featuring employees dressed head to toe as the Blue Man Group to an elaborate chase scene (with Asai as the quarry), these moments were carefully crafted to create sensorial peaks—ones that would enliven the experience in the moment and hang on the wall to continue defining the values long after the moment had passed.

This chapter has been chock-full of examples of companies punctuating company gatherings with levity to create peaks—and you know the four archetypes that will disproportionately help you in ensuring that these come alive.

But what about "ends"?

When Gina Amaro Rudan started as "Cultural Alchemist" at Google X, the company's secretive research and development facility that pursued bold, ambitious, seemingly impossible problems, she knew that the team needed a ritual for death—the death of work projects, that is.

Building on well-known ceremonies like Día de los Muertos (the Day of the Dead), Rudan conceived of "Dia X," what soon became an annual companywide celebration in which Google Xers build altars to the prototypes they've killed, deliver eulogies for the businesses they've shut down, and mourn the ideas they've laid to rest. They used levity to punctuate organizationally meaningful "ends."

On the surface, a Day of the Dead might seem like the opposite of lighthearted. But it became a surprisingly joyful way of reinforcing the cultural values of innovativeness and agility that were central to Google X's success. You need to "honor your idea, learn from it," Rudan says. "And we do that every year with a ritual."

But infusing levity into endings doesn't need to be a high-budget companywide affair, as one of our students' experiences illustrates. While at the Boston Consulting Group, he and his team were wrapping up a project for a particularly difficult client. As the project drew to a close, the team was left feeling tense and emotionally drained from the months of thankless work. So the project principal leading the engagement organized a team dinner and emceed an elaborate ceremony during which he gave each team member a "paper plate award" commemorating something funny that had happened during the project, on the back of a—you guessed it— flimsy paper plate.

As our student recalled, "It was a horrible project, but the team nevertheless ended up remembering it (and each other) rather fondly because of the ceremony. Pretty sure I still have that plate."

So remember: People remember peaks and ends. When your employees are asked about your organization's culture, when people approach them inquiring "What is it like to work there?" or "Why should I join?," they will draw upon their spikiest memories. Make sure they're good ones.

TURN ACCIDENTS INTO FOLKLORE

But designing new, humorous ceremonies and traditions is difficult for some. We get it. And we're here for you.

If these approaches aren't your bag, try instead to lean into your powers of *observation*. Look for *organic* moments of delight, and when you observe those that are resonant with the culture you aspire to have, either get out of the way or support them, and allow them to evolve.

At Ford Smart Mobility's Greenfield labs, where teams are working to discover and build mobility solutions for our tech-enabled transportation future, an engineer once remarked that some problems are "harder than putting socks on a chicken." Tickled by his choice of metaphor, the team instituted a weekly tradition of presenting one member with a pair of wild or weird (or chicken-bedazzled) socks as a way of acknowledging their work. The tradition soon became so integral that new hires and visitors to the lab are, to this day, welcomed into the fold with their own customized and often chicken-themed socks. So many socks are given out that they've become their own budget line item for the lab.

Rituals are the heart of an organization or team's culture. According to researcher Mike Norton at Harvard University, even seemingly odd rituals can become a source of group cohesion. By creating a sense of shared identity and goodwill, rituals inspire commitment, effort, and performance. They often take hold among a small team, then spread organization-wide, becoming so woven into the fabric of the culture that no one can remember a time before they existed.

Much like the most awe-inspiring comics, leaders with this ability are artful observers, keenly able to spot new behaviors or activities that they can formally incorporate into "official" organizational ceremonies—which is exactly what Joey Zwillinger did when an employee approached him with an odd bet.

Zwillinger is the CEO of the trendy sustainable footwear manufacturer, Allbirds. One day in August 2016, a member of the marketing team made a bet with him that they would reach $1.25 million in revenue by the end of that month. It was their sixth month in business and Allbirds was just coming off the retail seasonal lull in July alongside inventory shortages. Zwillinger found the number unreasonably high but played along. When he asked her what was on the line? "A frosé* machine for the office," she teased.

To both of their surprise, Allbirds hit the number. Zwillinger broadcast his loss and not only purchased a frosé machine, but in-

---

* Portmanteau term for "frozen rosé." In this entire book, this is our fanciest footnote.

stituted a weekly celebration; Frosé Fridays became a thing,* codifying this one-off joke into an ongoing tradition of levity.

In both these cases, new traditions arose organically, out of happy accidents. As a leader, you can encourage the formation of these spontaneous rituals by looking to your instigators and culture carriers—traditions that flow from the bottom up tend to be more widely and easily adopted, in our experience, than ones dictated from the top down. Look for *organic* moments of delight, support them, and then get out of the way.

The Walls Can Talk

What does your body language say about you right now?

Are your shoulders back or hunched? Is your mouth leaning more into a smile or a frown? Are you sitting proudly with your head high and chest forward like a royal? (One of the strong ones, not one of those frail Habsburgs.)

Body language speaks volumes. An organization's physical space is no different.

"Physical space is the body language of an organization," says Brendan Boyle, a principal at the global design firm IDEO. "When the verbal and physical language disagree—just like with our body language—the physical language reigns supreme."

There's a reason why tech giants like Google and Facebook hold their meetings in conference rooms with names like "We Didn't Start the Firefox,"† "Steven Tyler's Scarf," and "Toxicated": It sends

---

*That is, a thing most of the team regretted on most Saturdays.

†Upon hearing this fact, our friend David Iscoe disappeared for an hour without explanation and emerged with this: a set of historically accurate song lyrics to the tune of "We Didn't Start the Fire." Enjoy:

"We Didn't Start the Firefox" *by David Iscoe*
NCSA, Mosaic, Erwise tanked, it's archaic
Marc Andreesen, James Clark, Barksdale CEO
Netscape Navigator, Godzilla looked like a gator

playful cues to employees, as subtle as a small smile, that levity is welcome.

By now, we've all heard the tales about tech giants' over-the-top work environments, flush with ping-pong tables, trampolines, and colorful slides connecting conference rooms (yes, this is actually a thing).

While turning your office space into a veritable playground can indeed create a breeding ground for levity (and for class action lawsuits), it is by no means the only way. Research has shown that a range of environmental factors—from greater employee autonomy over workspace design to elements as simple as plants and bright colors—can promote engagement, productivity, creativity, and well-being. Work by Justin Berg, an organizational psychologist at Stanford University, shows that the "primal mark"—that is, the first visual cue an employee sees as they generate ideas—anchors the trajectory of novelty and usefulness. When the primal mark is surprising or unusual, creativity often follows.

Indeed, some of the most effective and profound alterations to physical space that we observed were the simplest—small, ever-present winks interwoven throughout physical space that constantly signal "We're here to work, but also to play."

For example, when the leaders of JibJab were first designing the

---

Number one market share, killer IPO
Netscape sold to AOL, product support went to hell
iPlanet, disbanded, nowhere left to go
AOL went bad to worse, Mozilla went open source
Foundation, Corporation, deprecated suite
Firefox, Thunderbird, friendly hackers spread the word
Bugzilla, Gecko, Pocket if you read
We didn't start the Firefox
It's as old as trousers
Since the world's had browsers
We didn't start the Firefox
No, we didn't code it
But our iPhones load it

office space at their Los Angeles headquarters, they decided to create and hang a series of enormous signs displaying the company's
values, one of which read AGILITY. Or, more accurately, it was *supposed to* read AGILITY. What it actually said was AGLITITY. Oops.
But cofounders Gregg and Evan Spiridellis decided to keep the mis-
spelled sign and display it in all its glory as a reminder that the
company embraces failure and doesn't take itself too seriously.

Designing a space for levity can go a long way toward reinforcing
crucial organizational values. IDEO is a master at this craft, whether
it's by encouraging employees to answer funny or thought-provoking
prompts posted on the walls, or randomly planting odd surprises
throughout the office, like a mini-golf hole at the base of the toilet.
At Forrester, a team created a wall of "quotes of the week" where
they would document the funniest moments and phrases, encouraging all employees to be on the lookout for moments of humor and
joy throughout the workday. And in 2014, when Tesla announced
they would be releasing all of their patents to the public, they com-
memorated this significant milestone by proudly displaying a play
on a popular meme, reading ALL OUR PATENT ARE BELONG TO
YOU, on a massive wall in their factory.

At the end of the day, the specific physical modifications matter
far less than the precision with which they reflect the unique values
and personality of the company culture—the lodestars of what the
company is and aspires to be.

Back at Pixar, we're shepherded around the office by Ed Catmull
as creatives flutter around their office spaces—which include elabo-
rately decorated desks and even a few little private huts. As longtime Pixar animator and director Brad Bird describes it: "If you
walk around downstairs in the animation area, you'll see that it is
unhinged. One guy might build a front that's like a Western town.
Someone else might do something that looks like Hawaii."

As we pass one office, we notice the outline of an archway drawn
on the wall. Noticing our confusion, Ed explains: Pixar has always

kept office walls white—a blank canvas so the animators could draw all over them. At one point, an employee took it a bit further, cutting an enormous archway into the wall so he could watch people walk by from the comfort of his own office. Though that employee had since moved on and the next occupant had the hole in the wall filled in, they paid him homage by having an outline of the archway drawn on the wall where the real thing used to be (a work hazard if they ever hire Wile E. Coyote).

This attitude toward office personalization at Pixar is emblematic of Catmull's philosophy of levity in the workplace: "Organic implies a beginning and an end," says Catmull. "We need to let our traditions grow, evolve, and die organically to make room for new ones."

Traditions, in Catmull's view, are things to hold on to lightly; some will fade away, and others will rise to take their place. Just like the archway in that office, leaders must hold respect for the old traditions while letting them fade away so that new ones can emerge. They must trust that they've planted the right seeds and enabled the right people, so that new rituals, traditions, and elements in their physical space will take shape.

CHAPTER 7

Navigating the Gray

Areas of Humor

"Humor plays close to the big hot fire, which is the truth. And the reader feels the heat."

—E. B. White

If you've ever had a disagreement about whether something is funny with a friend, colleague, or partner (who you then look at in bed that night while they're asleep, clutching a pint of Ben & Jerry's as a single tear runs down your face, wondering whether your mother was right and you've made a monumental mistake), this chapter is for you. It's about differences in the perception of humor, what causes them, how they play out, and what to do when they happen.

We all have different tastes and sensibilities when it comes to humor. You might think *Schitt's Creek* is the most brilliant show ever to grace the airwaves, while your best friend thinks it's "just okay." Maybe you think political humor is too taboo to bring into the office, whereas your co-worker is constantly impersonating the current occupant of the Oval Office. Or maybe your seventeen-year-old daughter is obsessed with a YouTube channel or a Twitch stream you find utterly inscrutable.*

---

* Or maybe your dad thinks a good pun lightens the day, while you think the only good pun is the one that never sees the light of day. Or your friend loves *South Park* for being an "equal opportunity offender," whereas you think two dozen wrongs don't make a right. Or your sister thinks jokes about people falling flat on their face (literally or metaphorically) are obnoxious, but you've fallen on yours so many times you need to joke about it. Or you find the antics of the gang on *Friends* delightful, or maybe, like the *Futurama* character Lrrr of planet Omicron Persei 8, you wonder—"Why does Ross, the largest Friend, simply not eat the other five?" Or maybe you're amused by Mr. Bean walking around with a turkey on his head, while your spouse just

MOST HUMOR WILL NOT LAND WITH EVERYONE

ha ha ha

■ PEOPLE WHO THOUGHT IT WAS FUNNY

☐ eh

The point is, what we find funny—or appropriate—is far from universal. There are a whole lot of gray areas when it comes to humor.

When we ask people what holds them back from using humor at work, many say it's the fear of inadvertently crossing a line. They aren't wrong to have this worry; in the workplace, inappropriate or aggressive humor (like teasing—in the wrong context or with the wrong person) can weaken relationships rather than strengthen them, getting in the way of resolving workplace conflict.*

Moreover, in our current era of heightened sensitivities, political polarization, and cancel culture, using humor at work can feel riskier than ever. As you've probably figured out by now, we believe humor

---

doesn't think humans should wear poultry under any circumstances. Or maybe your friend loves the way Maria Bamford talks openly about depression, but the silliness of it makes it hard for you to get on board. Maybe you love *BoJack Horseman* because it's full of animal puns, while your cousin loves it because it's a searingly accurate portrait of mental illness (softened by animal puns). Or maybe you read our footnotes because you are rigorous and know the value of hard work. Thank you; we see you and appreciate you.

*It's worth noting that Don Rickles never had an office job.

is a critically important tool to have on hand. But that doesn't mean it's always an easy or simple one to wield. In this chapter, we dive into when and why humor fails, and what to do when that happens.

We'll start by looking at the gray areas of humor—and how to walk the line. Then we'll dive into the lifecycle of a humor fail—how to recognize when you've bombed (hint: it's more complicated than simply listening for laughs), diagnose the situation, and make it right.

The goal is to wield humor responsibly: with sensitivity, empathy, and hilarity all working together. By understanding its nuances, we can make humor feel less risky *and* more versatile.

The Gray Areas of Humor

A little over halfway through the quarter in class, we do an activity called Spectrum. Here's how the Spectrum Activity works:

We show our students a series of jokes or comments made in various public forums that were presumably intended by the author or creator to be funny—tweets, ads, comics, videos, speeches made by public figures, and so on.

After each piece is shared, we ask the students to reflect, silently, on how each one landed in terms of "appropriateness" and "funniness". Next comes the fun part. Then students physically line themselves up,* stretching from "completely appropriate" on one side of the room to "completely inappropriate" on the other, and from "funny" to "not funny."

Once the lineup is set, the group discusses the way the reactions shook out and why people placed themselves where they did. For many of the prompts, we get a surprisingly wide range of responses—

---

*OR, if you are teaching this class online, they digitally line themselves up using tiny student avatars.

which is why it's crucial our students understand that the goal of the Spectrum exercise isn't to prove anyone wrong. It's to show that humor affects different people in many different ways, and that what constitutes appropriate versus inappropriate humor is, in most cases, highly subjective—a product of a host of factors including our personal experiences, backgrounds, settings, political leanings, level of hangriness, and more.

The rules of the activity guide the discussion: React first (don't analyze); Be open and honest; Own being an outlier; Celebrate shifts. The conversation is rich and candid, delving into topics of ethics, intent, and consequences. Students listen to each other's viewpoints, share personal experiences, and are given the opportunity to shift their position on the spectrum if they choose.

The activity often unearths uncomfortable realities, and the difficulty of these conversations is what makes them poignant. By prompting these conversations, our goal is to cultivate empathy, awareness, and, hopefully, behavior change.

So the question is: How do we take this range of likely responses into account as we attempt to build humor into our work and life? How do we walk the line without tumbling over it?

TRUTH, PAIN, DISTANCE

Our friend Anne Libera, a longtime director at The Second City theater and a professor at Columbia College Chicago who oversees the first B.A. degree in Comedy Writing and Performance in the United States, has a theory of comedy that helps shed some nuance on the gray areas of humor. Her theory looks at comedy as having three key components: truth, pain, and distance. Like our three branches of government (theoretically, anyway), these three parts operate in concert: If dialed correctly, they are the source of brilliant humor; if misapplied, they can offend and divide. So understanding them is key to being able to shift your humor according to context, status, and situation—and also understanding, in retrospect, why your humor may have crossed the line.

Truth is the heart of comedy. We laugh at what we recognize. At the same time, truth coupled with pain and not enough distance may come across as insensitive, hurtful, or offensive.

Pain can be physical or emotional. It can range from a moment of mild embarrassment or awkwardness to severe tragedy or trauma. (Libera defines pain more broadly to include elements like taboo, risk, and cognitive dissonance, but for our purposes, just know that this dimension usually involves some level of discomfort.) In some cases, finding the humor in our pain can be cathartic; in others, it can bring up old feelings we'd rather not relive.

Distance is a measure of how far an individual or group of people is from the subject of your humor. It can be temporal ("too soon" to laugh about something), geographic (whether something happened to me or my neighbor versus someone halfway across the world), or psychological (how relevant something is to our personal experience).

THE SPECTRUM

Let's revisit the Spectrum exercise to see how these three elements interact.

First, we showed our students a tweet. It read

> *"Cisco just offered me a job! Now I have to weigh the utility of a fatty paycheck against the daily commute to San Jose and hating the work."*

This tweet was clearly intended to be funny. But was it appropriate?

A student who found it perfectly harmless noted that she imagined this person had a private twitter account that only the tweeter's friends could see. Her rating of "appropriate" was founded on her belief that it's healthy and important to be able to vent to your friends about your frustrations—and therapeutic to do so with levity!

Meanwhile, on the "completely inappropriate" side of the room, another student provided a different perspective: What if this had been tweeted publicly instead? "The tweeter is essentially making fun of the company that he or she is about to join," the student pointed out. "If I were a Cisco employee, I'd be offended and frankly would question why we're hiring her."

Bingo.

It's easy to see the **truth** in this statement: It gets to the heart of the trade-offs we're all forced to make when it comes to work-life balance.* But if you remove the humor from the tweet, the writer was essentially saying, "Working at Cisco sucks, and if it didn't come with a big paycheck, I would never even consider taking this job."

This may be appropriate to say to a friend, but probably not to the entire Twittersphere—especially given that the company you're saying sucks almost certainly has a Twitter account and could easily get wind of your wisecrack.

It was in fact a public tweet, and a Cisco employee did see it. The truth stung, and ultimately the tweeter's offer was rescinded.

But using humor to shine light on painful truths is not always taboo. Take Cards Against Humanity, a popular party game known for being irreverent, edgy, and at times† politically incorrect. Launched via a Kickstarter campaign in 2009, the bestselling game has since expanded with special editions including the Geek Pack,

---

* Anyone who hasn't made a work-life trade-off either doesn't have a job, or doesn't have a life. Or has perfect versions of both, in which case we're jealous.

† Any time the game is played as intended.

the '90s Nostalgia pack, and Cards Against Humanity for Her—
a version of the game that parodies the existence of "for her" products, as explained in their FAQs:

Q: I already have Cards Against Humanity. Do I need this?

A: Treat yourself! Say yes to the dress. Find the best color to
wear for your skin tone. Stay in with the girls.

Q: What's different about it?

A: The box is pink, but the cards are exactly the same as the
original Cards Against Humanity. Sooo random.

Q: But why is it $5 more?

A: Because we're worth it.

The brand's satire isn't confined to the physical game itself; it
carries over to their website and marketing, as in the case of this ad:

veryone hates it when the men retire to the parlor to
iscuss the economy and the various issues of the day.
What are us ladies supposed to do?

Iow there's an answer. **Cards Against Humanity for
Her.** It's exactly the same as the original Cards Against
Iumanity game, but the box is pink and it costs
5 more.

Buy Now for $30

When we show this in class, we are rarely surprised that far more women than men find the gag funny. It makes sense. Women are more likely to recognize the truth in this joke: that products marketed as being "for women" are often more expensive than the *exact same thing** marketed as "for men" (like clothing, hair care products, skin care products, razors, dollars . . .).†

But what about the insinuation that men spend their evenings engaged in deep debate about matters like the economy and current events, while the women, after bringing the men their cigars and whiskey, retire to the kitchen to compare shopping lists? Were the women (or men) in our class offended? For the most part, no— because the satire was so clear. Almost everyone in the class deemed this ad appropriate because it's so exaggerated that there's no room for ambiguity about whether it's a joke.

"This is hilarious and speaks truth to an important issue," said one student, while another noted that "it's a powerful statement to make and this is a powerful way to do it." For our students, at least, the truth of the ad didn't sting, because its intent was so clear: to poke fun at certain realities of sexism, not to endorse them.

Pain and **distance** are closely linked in that the degree of distance often predicts how painful the topic will be for a given audience. If something tragic happened to you, a friend, a neighbor, your dog, your neighbor's dog, your dog's neighbor—the pain will be more live for you than for someone watching it on the news with no personal association to the people. Or dogs.

At the same time, the joke teller's distance from a topic is also

---

* Q: "When I inevitably purchase this without reading carefully and then find out it's the same cards as the original Cards Against Humanity, can I return it and get my money back?"
A: "That color looks great on you! No."

† It's called the pink tax, and if you hire a male accountant, at above-market rates, he'll tell you how to save on it.

an indication of how appropriate that topic is to joke about. Which is why the few students who were on the fence about this ad's appropriateness said essentially: It depends on who wrote it. "Ingroup" membership generally comes with permission to say certain things that someone who isn't a member of that group doesn't get. Intuitively this makes sense—women can make jokes about women that men cannot, older people can make jokes about the elderly that a young person can't, etc. So it follows that students would find the Cards Against Humanity for Her ad more appropriate if they knew it was written by a group of smart, funny women—whereas they might find it mean-spirited coming from a man.

Satire is a powerful tool for exposing—and coping with—painful realities in our world. But are there some things just *too* painful, or that hit *too* close to home to joke about? And how do we know when it's "too soon" to joke about them?

That's the conversation that inevitably ensues when we ask our students to reflect on the front page of *The Onion*'s 9/11 issue, published just two weeks after the attacks. During those dark weeks, not only did it feel too soon to laugh, many worried that comedy—and *The Onion*–style satire in particular—might be over for good.

On the surface, making light of the 9/11 attacks so soon after they occurred seems astonishingly insensitive, and clearly inappropriate. An untold number of Americans were mourning spouses, siblings, friends, cousins, co-workers, parents . . . and on top of it all, the country appeared to be heading to war. The pain was intense, and the distance nonexistent.

And yet when we asked our students (most of whom were in high school or college in 2001), many felt that the front page headlines captured the shock, devastation, and helplessness people experienced with a perfectly calibrated satirical twist—headlines like HOLY F##KING SH#T: ATTACK ON AMERICA and NOT KNOWING WHAT ELSE TO DO, WOMAN BAKES AMERICAN-FLAG CAKE. The reasons they gave—like the response of one student, who is from New York and was attending school there at the time, "It gave me some comic relief when I desperately needed it to help me process something unimaginable"—are poignant reminders that sometimes, the more we hurt, the more we need to laugh.

Of course, remembering one's reaction to a tragedy is one thing, but nineteen years between the tragedy and current day is a significant distance. However, digging into the public's reaction to the issue at the time tells a surprisingly similar story, largely because *The Onion*'s writers set a carefully crafted tone. Had they not, the high level of pain and the low distance from it could likely have led to starkly different responses.

For instance, the headline HUGGING UP 76,000 PERCENT is sweet and poignant, elevating the fact that people are coming together in a difficult time. The comedians are not joking about the pain, they're joking about the love.

Meanwhile, MASSIVE ATTACK ON PENTAGON PAGE 14 NEWS acknowledges the severity of a situation in which a major attack on the Pentagon would take a backseat. This severity is something almost everyone can agree on; it's not controversial.

As an article published in *Wired* magazine just a day after the issue was released summed it up: "Rather than coming off as insensitive, the satire tells a bitter truth: The problem is complicated, the danger real, and the future uncertain."

While you may not be tweeting jokes about your employer, creating products that battle gender inequality, or attempting to provide comic relief to a nation after tragedy, these principles help provide a framework for better understanding the humor you're putting into the world—and the levers at play when one audience versus another assesses its appropriateness. This isn't a hard-and-fast formula. The gray areas of humor are confusing, messy, and constantly shifting. So the best you can do when trying to navigate them is to keep the following in mind:

- **Examine the truth:** What if you remove the humor from the truth? Does the comment still feel appropriate to share in this context and to this audience?

- **Consider the pain and distance:** How great is the pain? Is it distant enough to laugh about? Or does it hit too close to home? Am I close enough to this person or group—or do I have enough personal experience with the source of the pain—to feel confident joking about it?

- **Read the room:** Reading the room isn't just about trying to understand what will make your listeners laugh. It's also about trying to understand how it will make them feel. Are people in the mood to take a joke? Are there cultural differences or other circumstances to take into account?

The Life Cycle of a Humor Fail

Thomas was the CEO of a small digital media company with around thirty full-time employees, and he had a problem employee—we'll call her Jackie. Everyone on Jackie's team had let Thomas know in no uncertain terms that Jackie was not performing up to the standards of the team—showing up late and leaving early each day, missing deadlines, not following through on important tasks. More than that, the team felt Jackie's demeanor was destructive to team culture; she talked down to team members and got angry when she was called out for missing deadlines. For a number of months, Thomas gave Jackie specific and actionable feedback. But when it became clear that she was still not improving, Thomas made the hard choice to fire her.

"Everybody had felt it coming for a while, but it was still a hard decision. We're a small team, so everybody knows and cares for everybody." And so while the change in some ways brought a collective sigh of relief, it also created some sadness—and some stress.

The team was worried that they would now be inheriting Jackie's workload (there were no immediate plans to replace her). What's more, while most people were aware of the reasons for Jackie's departure, as with a firing at any small company, it raised some trepidation around whether others' jobs might be in jeopardy as well.

The first big team meeting following the firing was one that Jackie normally led, and her absence was palpable. So in an effort to cut the tension, Thomas opened the meeting by joking, "Take it away, Jackie!" And then promptly wished *he* could be taken away . . . from the terrible atmosphere he'd just created.

After a few nervous chuckles, the room fell silent. Then one courageous employee stood up and said: "I don't think that's funny."

Thomas had deployed a major humor bomb. And he realized it immediately.

"It was a learning moment for me," Thomas later reflected, realizing that a more productive response to the tension in the room would have been to talk openly about what had happened, ask how everyone was feeling, and try to assuage the team's anxiety. But it was too late for any of that now.

Thomas acted swiftly and decisively to rectify his ill-timed joke. He gathered his thoughts and declared "You're absolutely right. I'm so sorry." Thomas acknowledged that his joking had come from a desire to ease the tension, but that it wasn't the moment—or the right way—to do that. His apology was sincere and immediate.

The response from his employees? One jumped in: "That's okay. You can start over if you want." Others in the room nodded in agreement.

And so he did. From the beginning.

This time, he opened the meeting with a heartfelt acknowledgment of Jackie's departure: how it would impact people from a workload perspective and how grateful he was to everyone on the team. He invited people to chime in with concerns, which he addressed with candor and empathy. And when the time felt right, he moved on to the planned agenda for the meeting.

Recovering from a humor fail is a three-step process. The first is simply to recognize that it happened. Second, you need to diagnose what went wrong, and finally, you need to rectify, or make it right. Let's look at how this played out for Thomas.

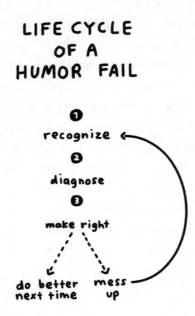

STEP ONE: RECOGNIZE

Thomas is, by all accounts, a brilliant, successful executive and not someone who is prone to making gaffes in public. And yet, despite good intentions, he found himself guilty of an egregious humor misfire. Why do so many smart, experienced, and well-intentioned people get this wrong?

There are three main reasons why recognizing the signals of appropriateness gets harder as you rise in rank:

1. The bounds of appropriateness are constantly shifting.

Appropriateness is a moving target, both for each of us individually as we rise in our careers and for all of us collectively as members of a constantly evolving society.

On a societal level, humor is like a litmus test for illuminating the cultural boundaries of propriety, often by pushing on them. These lines are very different than they were twenty or thirty years ago, and even ten or five years ago. Watch an episode of *Friends* or *Will & Grace* (or your favorite show from an earlier decade) to experience this point firsthand: What we remember as fun-loving, innocent, and playful humor can now smack of insensitivity, with stereotypes about race, gender, sexuality, and culture, to name just a deplorable few.

On a personal level, it's obvious that not all jokes you make around the dinner table will land in the office—and as humans, we get good at context switching. What's less obvious is how appropriateness shifts with power—that is, the jokes you made as a middle manager may not land when you're the CEO. In interview after interview, we've observed leaders struggle with the relationship between their humor and status.

Why is this such a pervasive trap that leaders in particular find themselves in?

2. As you rise in relative status, certain targets of humor become off-limits.

When you "punch up"—that is, tease someone of higher status—you can seem brave and confident. But "punch down" by making fun of someone of lower status, and you can seem like a jerk or a bully.

"At Google and Twitter, I was almost always punching up," says April Underwood, who, following her stints at these companies, became chief product officer at Slack. Earlier in her career, her humor could be irreverent, sometimes subtly pointing out an elephant in the room, she says. Taking jabs at more senior members of the team made her seem confident and actually helped her climb in status in a significant way. "As one of the more junior people in the room at most times, my sense of humor allowed me to spar with colleagues in a way that brought levity to a situation, humanized the leaders in the room, and signaled that I had their 'permission' to speak the truth in a way that was beneficial."

But at Slack, where Underwood reported straight to the CEO, and managed a team of up to 100 people, she had almost nowhere to punch up. "I quickly realized that that same kind of humor wasn't going to build trust, and it could even be scary to employees who were intimidated by me or my role," she says. "I felt I'd lost an important tool that got me here. I had to figure out what humor looked like for me as the boss in the room. I am still working on figuring it out."

Often, "humor from the top" takes the form of self-deprecation. That's because the higher you go, the more likely it is that making fun of anyone else will be "punching down."

At the same time, self-deprecation is a way for leaders to show they are confident enough to poke fun at their flaws. So for leaders, self-deprecation not only projects humility, making you more relatable and approachable, it can also *enhance* status and power.

(Note: Conversely, when people of lower status self-deprecate, it can further *diminish* perceptions of their status, because others are more likely to interpret their comments as insecurity. So the rule of thumb is: As you move up the old totem pole, make fun of others less, and yourself more.)

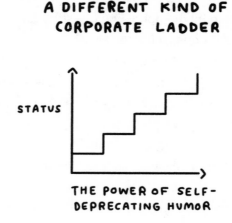

A DIFFERENT KIND OF CORPORATE LADDER

STATUS

THE POWER OF SELF-DEPRECATING HUMOR

3. The more status and power you gain, the harder it is to stay calibrated.

We're used to using other people's laughter as a barometer for the success (and appropriateness) of our humor. But as we gain power and authority, this barometer loses its accuracy. That's because laughter and social hierarchy are inextricably tied.

To illustrate, consider the joke:

Two muffins are baking in an oven. One of them yells, "Wow, it's hot in here!" And the other muffin replies: "Holy cow! A talking muffin!"

A group of social psychologists, Tyler Stillman, Roy Baumeister, and Nathan DeWall at Florida State University unleashed this Grade A dad joke on two groups of unsuspecting participants, priming one to feel more powerful than the interviewer and the other to feel subordinate. In the study, the joke was far more likely to elicit laughter when delivered to "subordinates."

Of course, it makes sense that appeasing the boss is a strategic move (and a survival tactic for our early ancestors). But as social creatures, we don't just laugh from a conscious desire to ingratiate ourselves—it's more hardwired than that. We know this because researchers ran the same experiment on a *new* set of unlucky subjects, only this time, participants heard the joke via prerecorded video, so they knew that the joke teller couldn't see or hear their response. Here again, those who believed the joke teller to be higher status were far more likely to laugh—even though the joke teller had no way of knowing who had laughed and who had not.

In short, when you make a joke from on high, people's laughter is often less a response to the joke itself than a reaction to status and hierarchy. Maybe you're funny, or maybe you're just the boss.* As Steve Reardon puts it, "Being CEO has opened my eyes to the fact that people will laugh at any stupid rubbish you say." This can make it exceptionally difficult for leaders to accurately calibrate the impact of their humor.

AM I FUNNY?

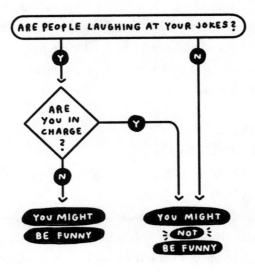

---

* Fade in: A woman finishes her toast at a company holiday party. As laughter fills the bar, she turns to the camera and slow-motion winks, as the familiar jingle fades in. "Maybe she's born with it. Maybe she's just the boss."

In Thomas's case, the deadly silence was the first clear signal of his humor misfire (the second was when someone literally told him to his face). He was lucky that his organization was still small and relatively nonhierarchical—so while his joke was met with a few nervous chuckles at first, the group quickly overcame the status differential to reveal a genuine response.

Unfortunately, we don't always get such clear signals. And in the same way that it's quite difficult to be aware of our own lack of awareness, in the absence of external data, we may be totally oblivious to the fact that our humor has crossed a line. If you're not getting accurate feedback, how can you be expected to adjust?

When we asked Seth Meyers for his single most important piece of advice to our students, it was to get good at recognizing this difference: "I'm pretty good at clocking the difference between when I'm really laughing and when I'm polite laughing," he told us. "The more you can recognize it in yourself, [the more] you'll recognize it in other people, too."

In short, there are a few ways to recognize a humor fail: You know because someone says something, you know because no one laughs, or everyone laughs but you're wise enough to check yourself (and your status). The learning here is to be aware of the status dynamics at play and not take the authenticity of the laughter as a given.

STEP TWO: DIAGNOSE

So you really blew it. What now? It's worth taking a moment to figure out *why* the humor failed.

In Thomas's case, the problem was twofold. First, he failed to read the room. He inaccurately gauged whether it was the right moment to make people laugh as well as how his particular joke would make them feel: an empathy fail as much as a humor fail. Had he taken a moment to check in on his colleagues' emotional state, he would likely have realized that no one was in the mood to laugh about Jackie's leaving.

Second, he punched down, making fun of someone lower in the ranks from his position of power. Because of the relationship between humor and status, punching down is something that everyone—and leaders in particular—needs to watch out for.

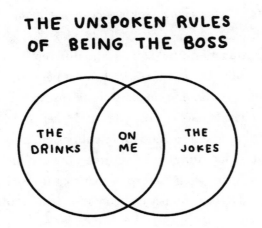

THE UNSPOKEN RULES OF BEING THE BOSS

THE DRINKS | ON ME | THE JOKES

Of course, misreading the audience or the status structure at play within it, as Thomas did, are by no means the only ways for humor to fail. A few other common mistakes to keep an eye out for include:

- **Knowing what jokes you can't tell.** Just as some students questioned whether the Cards Against Humanity ad was written by women, some jokes are best left to those most affected by the pain and distance. In 2016, *Late Night with Seth Meyers* added a simple but profound segment called "Jokes Seth Can't Tell." The segment starts with Meyers sitting between two of his brilliant writers, and kicks off like this—Amber Ruffin: "I'm black!" Jenny Hagel: "I'm gay!" Ruffin: "And we're both women!" Meyers:

". . . and I'm not!" Ruffin and Hagel then deliver the punch lines to, as Meyers puts it, "jokes that due to my being a straight white male would be difficult for me to deliver." Identity-based humor is always risky, which is why we would all be smart to follow what the *Moth* has established as the number one rule for their storyslam* events: Don't make another person's identity the prop, plot point, or punch line. *In short: Maybe your humor failed because you weren't the one who should be making the joke in the first place.*

- **Minding your medium.** Things land differently in person than via text. While this seems obvious, most people are worse than they think at switching media. In one research experiment by Justin Kruger, Nicholas Epley, Jason Parker and Zhi-Wen Ng, subjects were asked to send an email designed to evoke a particular emotional tone and then rate how confident they were that the recipient would interpret that tone accurately. Surprise! They tended to be seriously overconfident in assuming that their sarcasm would be understood. *In short: Maybe your humor failed because its meaning was lost in the medium.*

- **Context switching.** It goes without saying that humor is context dependent; jokes that work in the living room won't necessarily land in the boardroom. At work, keep it PG-13. That means *The Avengers, Jumanji,* and *Kindergarten Cop.* If you're at work, don't say it unless Arnold Schwarzenegger would say it in front of a bunch of five-year-olds. *In short: Maybe your humor failed because you failed to context switch.*

---

*Despite the name, the storyslam bears no resemblance to a WWE event and is in fact more like an open mic night for stories. Though it would be kind of adorable if, during one WWE primetime event, Brock Lesnar pulled out a book instead of a folding chair and told everyone a heartbreakingly beautiful tale involving love, loss, and lower back muscles.

- **Avoiding your personal humor pitfall.** In chapter 1, we explored four broad humor styles. If you're on the aggressive side of the spectrum, what you view as intimacy-enhancing teasing might hurt or offend. If you're on the affiliative side, maybe you (like Thomas) used humor out of a desire to lighten the mood when you shouldn't have. *In short: Maybe you failed because you fell into a pitfall of your style.*

Whether we're failing to read the room, punching down, punching ourselves (when we shouldn't be), or making one of these many other gaffes, we're all going to miss the mark at one time or another. Is it deeply unpleasant? Yes. But it's also in the past. Which means that until science figures out time travel, you can't change it. All you can do is learn from it—and try to make it right.

STEP THREE: MAKE IT RIGHT

A wise piece of advice about what to do after a humor fail came to us from former CEO of DoSomething.org, Nancy Lublin: When you step over the line, get out the power washer.

The metaphor comes from a personal experience Lublin had years ago, which stuck with her. It was the night before her last day at DoSomething.org, and Lublin wanted to make a public gesture to her staff about how much she appreciated them. In what she intended as a lighthearted prank, Lublin had large stencils made that said things like "thank you for being awesome" and "this is what a leader looks like," and then she and a few members of her team drove all over Brooklyn, Queens, and Manhattan, stopping at each of their co-workers' homes so she could paint these phrases on the sidewalk, along with arrows to each of her employees' homes. The aim was to communicate gratitude and admiration, but Lublin didn't fully consider the ramifications.

One of her employees, Mike, was jarred by Lublin's prank. His landlord was quite particular about the property and took great pride in keeping it well-maintained—what's more, she lived in the unit upstairs. Mike was sincerely worried that his landlord would see Lublin's paint job before he had a chance to buy the supplies he'd need to wash it off. When Lublin heard this, she was mortified. After apologizing profusely to Mike, she jumped into action. Lublin tracked down a contractor in Brooklyn with a power washer and availability to clean Mike's sidewalk that day, and she reached out to other employees to ask if she could help them with cleaning as well. The contractor was so used to cleaning up nasty graffiti that when he arrived at Mike's home and saw what he was being hired to clean, he had a good laugh—and gave Lublin half off the price. He said he'd never cleaned up "love notes" before. By the end of the day, the sidewalk had been cleaned. Lublin had apologized, not just with words but with action. And she reflected years later on how this moment of shortsightedness had been an important lesson.

When humor fails or offends, it can be tempting to brush it off as the other person's problem—"he didn't get the joke" or "she's being too sensitive"—instead of stopping to consider how it might be *our* problem. In these moments, lean in: trust their reaction, understand and acknowledge your mistake, reflect on your blind spots, and make it right. Don't just apologize, get out the power washer.

HOW TO APOLOGIZE
(FOR A BAD JOKE AND BEYOND)

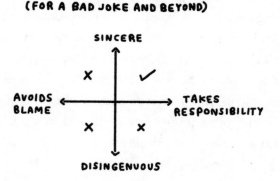

The Dangers of Superpowers: A Coda

If you believe, as we do, that humor is a superpower, we urge you to remember what every Marvel movie teaches us: that great power can be used for good . . . or, just as easily, for evil.

We don't mean to imply that you might be evil. Of course, nobody (except maybe Dr. Doom) gets up in the morning saying "Time to be evil."

It bears noting, though: Recognizing and rectifying *failed* humor is important. But recognizing *derogatory* humor is *critical*—not just for you as an individual, but for all of us as a society.

It's obvious that racist, sexist, and otherwise prejudiced humor is cruel, offensive, and unambiguously *not* appropriate, at work or anywhere. And yet most of us have experienced moments when humor crossed a line—where someone justified an off-color remark with "It was just a joke" or "Of course I don't actually believe that." And while it may feel easier and more comfortable to let these moments slide, there's real danger in remaining silent.

Research has shown that mere exposure to disparaging, identity-based humor is likely to perpetuate prejudice in those who are already predisposed to it.

As one study by researchers Robyn Mallett, Thomas Ford, and Julie Woodzicka found, when men who had (in prior tests) been found to hold sexist views* were told either a series of neutral jokes

---

*In the least fun footnote of this book, allow us to elaborate. These men tested high in what's called "hostile sexism" on the Ambivalent Sexism Inventory, which means they indicated agreement with statements like "The world would be a better place if women supported men more and criticized them less," "A wife should not be significantly more successful in her career than her husband," or "There are many women who get a kick out of teasing men by seeming sexually available and then refusing male advances."

or a series of sexist jokes;[*] those who heard the sexist jokes—relative to those who heard the neutral jokes—reported greater tolerance of gender harassment in the workplace and less remorse after being asked to imagine they had personally harassed a woman. In a similar study by researchers Thomas Ford, Christie Boxer, Jacob Armstrong, and Jessica Edel, sexist men who watched sexist comedy skits recommended bigger funding cuts to a women's organization than to other student organizations at their university, relative to those who watched non-sexist comedy. Similar findings hold true when the derogatory humor centers on issues of race, sexual orientation, and other areas of identity.

Put simply: Derogatory humor doesn't just push boundaries or highlight divisions. It can perpetuate prejudice and impact behavior by those with prejudice views. It further divides.

But what about the "Cards Against Humanity for Her" ad, you might be wondering? Totally sexist. Or the "Hijackers Are Surprised to Find Themselves in Hell" article from the 9/11 issue of *The Onion* leans on misperceptions about the Islamic faith. Are these divisive, or are they using humor as a tool to highlight the sheer absurdity of certain stereotypes?

The line isn't always clear. Ultimately, the difference comes down to not just the joke-teller, but the audience and why they're laughing. In other words, are people laughing at the obvious and deliberate ridiculousness of it—that is, the incongruity between reality and what is being said—or are they laughing because they think the stereotypes are true?

The danger in that tension comes from what Sarah Silverman has called the "mouthful-of-blood" laugh (or what *The Onion* founder Scott Dikkers has similarly dubbed "blood laughter"): the full-

---

[*] Such as: "A man and a woman were stranded in an elevator and they knew they weren't gonna make it out alive. The woman turns to the man and says, 'Make me feel like a woman before I die.' So he takes off his clothes and says, 'Fold them!'" Yeah, we know.

throated laugh from someone in the audience who interprets your off-color joke not as a critique or commentary on some abhorrent slur or stereotype, but as an endorsement of it. This is a real risk that comes with the territory, and it's why we are well-served to heed the *Moth*'s number one rule for their storyslam events: Don't make another person's identity the prop, plot point, or punch line.

This is not to say that we should be scared of using humor for fear of repercussions. (Quite the opposite—as we hope you've gleaned from the foregoing chapters illuminating the far-reaching power of humor.) Rather, it's our responsibility to navigate these gray areas with care. To stay calibrated to cultural and personal shifts, recognize and rectify mistakes, and understand the impact of our humor—especially when used as the powerful tool it is to shed light on issues of social injustice. In the words of bestselling author (and self-proclaimed Professional Troublemaker) Luvvie Ajayi, "We've got to get comfortable with being uncomfortable by speaking hard truths when they're necessary." Lean into the uncomfortable conversations when you hear humor that crosses a line—striving for empathy, awareness, and change.

In short: With great humor comes great responsibility.

Wield it for good.

Why Humor Is a

Secret Weapon in Life

"A sense of humor is needed armor. Joy in one's heart and some laughter on one's lips is a sign that the person down deep has a pretty good grasp of life."

—Hugh Sidey

You've come to the end of this book. You now know (we hope) how to infuse your work life with humor and levity, and why it's so important. But here's the thing: Once the workday is over, you go home to your full and beautiful and complicated life. What then?

As you know by now, Jennifer has spent the last two decades researching the drivers of human well-being: How do people create meaning in their lives, how is meaning different than happiness, and ultimately, how does one design a life well lived?

Much of that work was inspired by the regrets of the dying. Jennifer's ~~interest~~ preoccupation with death began early; her mother has been volunteering at hospice for nearly forty years, so Jennifer grew up hearing stories around the dinner table about the people her mother supported and what they wished for in their last days of life.*

In hearing about the wishes that people express in their final days, she began to notice they cluster around a few consistent themes: boldness, authenticity, presence, joy, and love.

Through our work together over the last six years, we have found that humor and levity are uniquely powerful tools for fulfilling each of these wishes—and thus for contributing to a life well-lived.

Don't get us wrong: We care about you becoming a badass business titan. We care about your bottom lines. We even care about your top lines.† But we care more about you as a whole person. We

---

* "We are what you call a super fun family."—Jennifer

† Note: not a thing.

care more about your opportunity to use the concepts in this book to live better, more fulfilling lives (that will one day conclude with no—or at least fewer—regrets).

So with that we end our journey together by merging these two different yet profoundly connected sides of our work: levity and a life well lived. In both, boldness, authenticity, presence, joy, and love flourish.

Boldness: *"I wish I had lived more fearlessly."*

Fear holds us back from making bold choices that can define our lives. So to live more boldly, we must first tackle fear. Which humor does. Not by making us more courageous or fearless—but by opening us up to change and possibility. Humor empowers us with the boldness to take bigger risks and helps us bounce back more quickly from setbacks—so we can dust ourselves off and try again.

I'm not funny. What I am is brave.

—*Lucille Ball*

Authenticity: *"I wish I had lived a life true to myself."*

Meeting or exceeding the expectations of others can be an intoxicating source of pride. But when we focus too much energy on reaching an outcome or portraying a certain version of ourselves, we can lose our grounding along the way. Humor empowers us to share parts of ourselves that are risky, unconventional, and authentic—thereby shifting others' expectations to ones that are more personally true, and providing the perspective to care less about ones that don't matter.

Don't waste your time trying to change opinions. Do your thing and don't care if they like it.

—*Tina Fey*

Presence: *"I wish I'd stopped to appreciate the moment more."*

Humor is a choice, one that requires you to watch carefully as your life is unfolding, listen to those around you, and be present in the moment. We are wired to reflect on our past and envision our future; humor helps remind us that each day—as it unfolds—is our life. By prompting us to search for hidden truths in each moment and to look at people and situations in a new light, humor engenders presence.

The last time doesn't exist. It's only this time... There's only now.

—*Bill Murray*

Joy: *"I wish I had laughed more—and not taken myself so seriously."*

Joy is not a happy accident, but a choice we make: a thing we allow ourselves to seek and find. It's about being more generous with your laughter and finding delightful moments in the day. When you don't take yourself too seriously—you laugh effortlessly. And that is when joy flows.

Do things that make you happy within the confines of the legal system.

—Ellen DeGeneres

Love: *"I wish I had the chance to say 'I love you' one more time."*

Where there is love, humor is not far behind. There are few tiny acts as easy and generous as sharing a laugh with someone—these moments, though fleeting, are tiny expressions of love. And by quickening the path to trust and self-disclosure, relationships are strengthened. When laughter cuts through tension and divisiveness to forge connection, humor and levity enable love.

*   *   *

Boldness, authenticity, presence, joy, and love: It is hard to imagine more rewarding life pursuits. And lucky for us (and our readership), each is deeply connected with humor. This is why we believe so strongly that a life of purpose and meaning is a life filled with laughter and levity.

In my experience, you will truly serve only what you love. If you love friends, you will serve your friends. If you love community, you will serve your community. If you love money, you will serve money. And if you love only yourself, you will serve only yourself, and you will have only yourself.

—Stephen Colbert

The End (of This Book)

We appreciate your going deep with us. We appreciate your wading through these heavier meditations on death and a life well lived, especially for those who may have picked up our book expecting page upon page of puns and rubber chickens.

Remember: Humor, in both work and life, begins with the subtlest of mindset shifts. It begins with movement.

So start moving.

Look closely for the sparks of levity in the nooks and crannies of your everyday experience (we promise they're there). Look for the invitations from your spouse or co-worker or cashier to engage and play.

And when you see these small sparks, instead of looking down at your phone, give them oxygen—fan them into flames, play along, and build on them. So that they spread and multiply, warming your colleagues and the loved ones around you. Even in moments of darkness. Especially in those moments.

Now imagine if everyone in the world had this mindset. Imagine if everyone searched for these sparks and spent more time walking through life on the precipice of a smile. Imagine that world. (Now let's create it.)

Thank you for being with us on this journey. And so that we don't regret not saying it later: we love you.

Michael: Okay, so, for this afterword, I think you should break the mold of how afterwords work.

Jennifer: Yes! We are anti-molds; totally down to break them. What are you thinking?

Michael: Keep it real simple and say, "We're going to end our book by interviewing someone *about* our book." Because who *does that* at the end of their book?

Naomi: You're a madman. We're in. Any other advice before we get started?

[Michael pauses . . . then points to the two corners of Naomi's living room.]

Michael: I would move that plant on the right over to the left, and move the one on the left to the right.

Naomi: You know what's crazy, I do that every night before I go to bed, and by the morning, they've always moved themselves back.

* * *

So, here's the deal. We're going to end our book by interviewing Michael Lewis *about* our book. Because who *does that*? This is that interview, and these are its words: the (after)words.

Jennifer: In the book, we talk (a lot) about the role that humor—and levity more broadly—can play in our work and in our lives. What role would you say humor and levity have played in your life?

Michael: My approach is just to always have fun. Most of the rich things in my life, even if they're hard, are a lot of fun, too. I find generally, the times when I'm feeling out of step with my own life—when I feel I'm not living properly—are when I'm having the least amount of fun.

So one of the ways I check to make sure that I'm living life the way I should is: if I notice long stretches without humor of any sort, I know something's wrong. It's like you're in the woods, and you have the sudden sense you're about to get eaten. You just know something feels wrong. And so I'll intentionally stop and notice it and disrupt whatever is happening.

Jennifer: So is humor a constant in your day-to-day?

Michael: It is. But here's the thing: Humor is not its own category—it's something that bleeds into all the other categories, as opposed to just being contained in this little comedy club in your mind. It's like salt on airplane food—it makes everything better. It has a place everywhere, not just at the beginning of a PowerPoint presentation.

I think most of the people who pick up this book are going to be people who think to themselves, "I need to be funny." But they're going to find out that that's not what they need. What they need is to introduce a totally different spirit into their lives. Maybe they feel right now like there's something they're missing out on, or they put up walls between themselves and other people, either consciously or inadvertently.

And this is a book that can help people get past that and tear down those walls.

Naomi: You mentioned to us earlier that you'd been curious about the topic of humor for a while. What sparked your interest in the first place?

Michael: One of the first thoughts I had when I heard about your work on humor is: What a fun inefficiency to explore.* That's one thing I love about this concept—the way you're taking a stand against this idea that either you've got it or you don't. The mind rebels at the idea of being able to teach it, because it feels so much like something that arises spontaneously in conversation. And it seems like something that's nature, not nurture. The only time I ever felt like it was a skill that could be taught was when I went to Second City to learn improv.

Jennifer: What prompted you to take classes at Second City— despite your mind rebelling at the idea?

Michael: So, at that point, my now eighteen-year-old was maybe eight. And at that age, she was insufferable. Negative about every- thing. You couldn't give her new foods, anything you proposed she tended to kind of reject. I thought—her life is the opposite of im- prov. And I thought—maybe if I could get a little "yes, and" into her life, it would change things for the better. So I enrolled her in a two-day kids' class, while I took a class for adults that ran at the same time. I remember coming out for lunch after three hours in

---

* Authors' note: "fun inefficiency."

class, and I was just drenched in sweat. Like, it was the most panic-inducing three hours I'd ever experienced. It was so hard. And my daughter came out of her class with a big smile on her face, and she said, "That was so fun! That was so easy!"

And I thought: this is the difference between kids and grown-ups. You don't realize how rigid you are in your head until you're forced into that situation. To this day, I try to remember it from time to time and respond to the world the way you would in an improv scene.

Naomi: One of the things I love about that story is your focus on mindset—on navigating the world in a different way. You once took on an experiment suggested by Dacher Keltner, where you wrote down three funny things at the end of each day. And even though you're a person who's constantly on the lookout for fun in your life, you said that the moment you had to write down what was funny, it got harder. When you sat down and you started looking for something specifically, then it's almost like you lost the magic. So how do you reconcile these two things—how do you find more humor in your life without looking for it?

Michael: Right, the moment I had to write the things down, it became a constraint. The things I wrote down felt less funny. It got so hard that the last day, I was asking my nineteen-year-old daughter to give me a list of all the funny things she could think of—so I could steal them.

It's sort of like where you landed this book. You zoom out and say "But really, this is not about being funny." You've learned all of these things, now hold them lightly and just shift your mindset toward the world. Don't try too hard, don't focus on the outcome. If you just shift your mindset in this one way, it will make your life better and richer in all these other ways.

And that's totally right. There's this book called *The Inner Game of Tennis* by Timothy Gallwey, which was the beginning of inner-game-like coaching back in the '70s. The three-sentence description of the book is: This guy coaching tennis is no longer telling people how to hit the tennis ball. He's telling them to focus on their core muscles, or their breath, or something other than how well they're hitting the tennis ball. Focus on something that's important, like what they're doing with their body, not the outcome.

If "being funny" is an outcome, and if you focus on that outcome too much—like if you're too much in your head and you start to focus on where the ball is going—you can lose the flow. Your mind is going to find something to focus on. Much better not to focus on being funny. Let the funny just take care of itself.

Jennifer: So be more focused on having fun than being funny. Did you always have this belief system?

Michael: Yes, I'd say this is the attitude people had where I grew up, in New Orleans. People there would say it's not important to be funny; it's important for people to feel like it's fun to be with you. And there are lots of ways to generate that feeling of, oh, man, it's nice to be with you. But it makes me better, it makes my work better. I often find that if I'm not having fun with a book or podcast or a screenplay, the audience is not having fun. People don't want to have a boring life, or even a boring conversation. They're just risk-averse. If you create an environment where there's no reason to be afraid, all of a sudden things loosen up.

Naomi: In the moments in your life where you feel like you're not having fun—when you're in the woods, about to get eaten—what do you do?

Michael: When I've been in those moments—where I had that sense of foreboding that, man, this has gotten tedious for some stretch of time—what I would usually do is cause trouble in some way. Here's an example: The other day, my wife and kids and I were about to sit down to dinner, and I was getting kind of an ominous feeling about where things were headed, because my kids were bickering. And meanwhile, I've been taking singing lessons. I don't sing, but I'm taking these lessons, and they involve voice training, where you do this incredibly crazy shit with your voice to try to broaden your range. So at the dinner table, over my kids bickering, I just started singing. Loudly. Doing these crazy vocal exercises. They've heard me do it at a distance, and it kind of creeps them out, so they instantly knew what I was doing and they stopped bickering immediately. It was totally bizarre. But it worked.

Using humor is like starting a fire. It's cold and dark where you are; you want to get it to warm up and be lighter. So you cause a little trouble. And as long as there is love behind that trouble, it lands as fun.

If you get in the habit of your life being fun, if you move through life believing it's supposed to be that way, you'll notice when it's not. I've been making life fun for so long I can't imagine putting up with no fun. But the inverse is true, too. If you get in the habit of life not being fun, you start to not even notice, because that's what you're used to.

Jennifer: One last thing before we leave you. At the end of the book, we talk about the relationship between love and humor—how sharing a laugh is a little expression of love. Is that something that's been true in your own life? Please say yes.

[slides $100 bill across the table]

Michael: Yes.

Emotion in general is a source of humor; whether it's love or hate or even sadness. Emotion causes you to pay close attention to something. But love in particular creates a very emotional space.

Last summer, I was asked to give a eulogy at a funeral—which was something I'd never done. So I got advice from someone who'd given many eulogies: "Just keep it simple." Simple statements stick with people in those situations. And when you make those simple statements and you're sincere about them, you heighten everyone's emotions.

So at the memorial, I said that I loved my friend, and I explained why I loved him, and I told stories about us. And here and there I inserted a little humor so things didn't stay too heavy. What I noticed was that everything was taken to be ten times funnier than it actually was, because people were already in that really emotional space.

So I'd say that if you've got love present—humor isn't that far behind.

HUMOR STYLES MINI QUIZ

The questions below are a quick, back-of-the-envelope way to get a sense of which humor style is closest to yours. To take the full humor styles quiz and learn more about your style and the styles of others, head to humorseriously.com.

humorseriously.com

STEP 1:

Read each statement and score yourself from 1 to 5, where 1 = "strongly disagree" and 5 = "strongly agree."

1. ____ My sense of humor is uplifting and wholesome; I am generous with laughter.
2. ____ While saying something humorous, I often deliver it while smiling or laughing.
3. ____ Others would describe my humor as animated, sometimes slapstick.
4. ____ My sense of humor is dark and edgy; you have to earn my laughter.
5. ____ When saying something humorous, I often deliver it with a straight face.
6. ____ Others would describe my humor as dry and sarcastic, an acquired taste.

7. _____ I enjoy being the center of attention when joking, and am confident riffing on the spot.

8. _____ My humor is bold, irreverent, and roasting; I'm not afraid to ruffle a few feathers to get a laugh.

9. _____ I have a thick skin for people making fun of me and don't mind being the butt of a joke.

10. _____ I prefer to plan out humor before I say it and am not interested in the spotlight.

11. _____ My humor is understated and modest; I carefully consider how my humor will land on others before saying it.

12. _____ I think that roasts, pranks, and teasing usually aren't worth the risk of hurt feelings.

STEP 2:

Add up your scores as indicated below, and circle the highest! The higher your score, the more likely you are to display characteristics of the corresponding humor style:

YOUR SCORE		STYLE
Sum of items 1–3:	_____	Magnet
Sum of items 4–6:	_____	Sniper
Sum of items 7–9:	_____	Stand-Up
Sum of items 10–12:	_____	Sweetheart

NOTES

Chapter 1: The Humor Cliff

22 **going over the humor cliff together**: At the bottom of that abyss we're joined by the majority of 1.4 million survey respondents in 166 countries who revealed in this Gallup poll that the frequency with which we laugh or smile each day starts to plummet around age twenty-three.

23 **average four-year-old laughs**: P. Gerloff, "Why You Need to Laugh Like a 5-Year-Old," *Huffpost,* June 22, 2011, https://www.huffpost.com/entry/laughter-and-health_b_881210.

24 **preferring employees with a sense of humor**: Hodge-Cronin & Associates, 1986, "Humor in Business: A Survey."

25 **lack of trust in leadership**: D. Sturt and T. Nordstrum, "10 Shocking Workplace Stats You Need to Know," *Forbes,* March 8, 2018, https://www.forbes.com/sites/davidsturt/2018/03/08/10-shocking-workplace-stats-you-need-to-know/#76e360b2f3af.

25 **leaders who use self-deprecating humor**: C. Hoption, J. Barling, and N. Turner, "'It's Not You, It's Me': Transformational Leadership and Self-Deprecating Humor," *Leadership & Organization Development Journal* 34(1), 2013, 4–19, doi: 10.1108/01437731311289947.

25 **supervisors' ratings of team performance**: N. Lehmann-Willenbrock and J. A. Allen, "How Fun Are Your Meetings? Investigating the Relationship Between Humor Patterns in Team Interactions and Team Performance," *Journal of Applied Psychology* 99(6), 2014, 1278.

27 **perceptions of status, competence, and confidence**: T. B. Bitterly, A. W. Brooks, and M. E. Schweitzer, "Risky Business: When Humor Increases and Decreases Status," *Journal of Personality and Social Psychology* 112(3), 2017, 431–55.

29 managers *with a sense of humor*: W. H. Decker, "Managerial Humor and Subordinate Satisfaction," *Social Behavior and Personality* 15(2), 1987, 225–32.

30 **174,000 Gallup respondents**: And the good news is that if you're anything like these 174,000 Gallup respondents, you're likely already doing this a lot more outside of the office than in it. So you've been practicing.

31 *growth mindset*: C. S. Dweck, *Mindset: The New Psychology of Success* (New York: Random House, 2006).

33 **a few shades darker**: R. Martin, P. Puhlik-Doris, G. Larsen, J. Gray, K. Weir. "Individual Differences in Uses of Humor and Their Relation to Psychological Well-Being: Development of the Humor Styles Questionnaire." *Journal of Research in Personality*. 37(1), 2003, 48–75.

Chapter 2: Your Brain on Humor

43 **cocktail of hormones (dopamine, cortisol, endorphins)**: J. Yim, "Therapeutic Benefits of Laughter in Mental Health: A Theoretical Review," *Tohoku Journal of Experimental Medicine* 239(3), 2016, 243–49.

43 **cocktail of hormones (oxytocin . . . endorphins)**: S. J. Nasr, "No Laughing Matter: Laughter Is Good Psychiatric Medicine," *Current Psychiatry* 12(8), 2013, 20–25.

46 **37 percent higher in status**: T. B. Bitterly, A. W. Brooks, and M. E. Schweitzer, "Risky Business: When Humor Increases and Decreases Status," *Journal of Personality and Social Psychology, 112*(3), 2017, 431–55.

47 **humorous replies to ridiculous questions**: D. P. Howrigan, K. B. Mac-Donald, "Humor as a Mental Fitness Indicator," *Evolutionary Psychology* 6(4), 2008, 147470490800600411.

48 **"and I'll throw in my pet frog"**: K. O'Quin, J. Aronoff, "Humor as a Technique of Social Influence," *Social Psychology Quarterly* (1981): 349–57.

49 **33 percent higher point value**: T. R. Kurtzberg, C. E. Naquin, and L. Y. Belkin, "Humor as a Relationship-Building Tool in Online Negotiations," *International Journal of Conflict Management* 2009.

49 **remembered more about current events**: "Public Knowledge of Current Affairs Little Changed by News and Information Revolutions," Pew Research Center, April 15, 2007.

49 **a brief short-term memory test**: G. S. Bains, L. S. Berk, N. Daher, E. Lohman, E. Schwab, J. Petrofsky, and P. Deshpande, "The Effect of

Humor on Short-Term Memory in Older Adults: A New Component for Whole-Person Wellness," *Advances in Mind-Body Medicine* 28(2), 2014, 16–24.

50 **11 percent higher on their final exams**: A. Ziv, "Teaching and Learning with Humor: Experiment and Replication," *Journal of Experimental Education* 57(1), 1988, 4–15.

50 **NPR surveyed its listeners**: "The State of the Union," *In Your Words*, NPR, January 25, 2011.

53 **30 percent more intimate**: A. W. Gray, B. Parkinson, and R. I. Dunbar, "Laughter's Influence on the Intimacy of Self-Disclosure," *Human Nature* 26(1), 2015, 28–43.

55 **23 percent more satisfied in their relationships**: D. G. Bazzini, E. R. Stack, P. D. Martincin, and C. P. Davis, "The Effect of Reminiscing About Laughter on Relationship Satisfaction," *Motivation and Emotion* 31(1), 2007, 25–34.

57 **Five-year-old children**: T. P. German and M. A. Defeyter, "Immunity to Functional Fixedness in Young Children," *Psychonomic Bulletin & Review* 7(4), 2000, 707–12.

58 **laughter helped them overcome their functional fixedness**: A. M. Isen, K. A. Daubman, and G. P. Nowicki, "Positive Affect Facilitates Creative Problem Solving," *Journal of Personality and Social Psychology* 52(6), 1987, 1122.

59 **The comedians' captions were better**: O. Amir and I. Biederman, "The Neural Correlates of Humor Creativity," *Frontiers in Human Neuroscience* 10, 2016, 597.

59 **25 percent more creative**: B. M. Kudrowitz, "Haha and aha!: Creativity, Idea Generation, Improvisational Humor, and Product Design," Massachusetts Institute of Technology PhD dissertation 2010.

60 **psychological safety**: A. Edmondson, "Psychological Safety and Learning Behavior in Work Teams," *Administrative Science Quarterly* 44(2), 1999, 350–83.

60 **The link between humor and psychological safety**: L. S. Berk, S. A. Tan, and D. Berk, "Cortisol and Catecholamine Stress Hormone Decrease Is Associated with the Behavior of Perceptual Anticipation of Mirthful Laughter," 2008.

61 **a correlation between lower cortisol**: B. K. Lee, T. A. Glass, M. J. McAtee, G. S. Wand, K. Bandeen-Roche, K. I. Bolla, and B. S. Schwartz, "Associations of Salivary Cortisol with Cognitive Function in the

Baltimore Memory Study," *Archives of General Psychiatry* 64(7), 2007, 810–18.

62 **workplace stress:** J. Goh, J. Pfeffer, and S. A. Zenios, "The Relationship Between Workplace Stressors and Mortality and Health Costs in the United States," *Management Science* 62(2), 2016, 608–28.

63 **increased satisfaction with their current social relationships:** D. Keltner and G. A. Bonanno, "A Study of Laughter and Dissociation: Distinct Correlates of Laughter and Smiling During Bereavement," *Journal of Personality and Social Psychology* 73(4), 1997, 687.

63 **fewer instances of depression:** S. A. Crawford and N. J. Caltabiano, "Promoting Emotional Well-being Through the Use of Humour," *Journal of Positive Psychology* 6(3), 2011, 237–52.

64 **increasing blood flow and muscle relaxation:** M. Miller and W. F. Fry, "The Effect of Mirthful Laughter on the Human Cardiovascular System," *Medical Hypotheses* 73(5), 2009, 636–39.

64 **reducing the arterial wall stiffness:** C. Vlachopoulos, P. Xaplanteris, N. Alexopoulos, K. Aznaouridis, C. Vasiliadou, K. Baou, . . . and C. Stefanadis, "Divergent Effects of Laughter and Mental Stress on Arterial Stiffness and Central Hemodynamics," *Psychosomatic Medicine* 71(4), 2009, 446–53.

64 **experienced improved lung function:** M. H. Brutsche, P. Grossman, R. E. Müller, and J. Wiegand, "Impact of Laughter on Air Trapping in Severe Chronic Obstructive Lung Disease," *International Journal of Chronic Obstructive Pulmonary Disease* 3(1), 2008, 185.

64 **a fifteen-year longitudinal study:** S. Romundstad, S. Svebak, A. Holen, and J. Holmen, "A 15-Year Follow-up Study of Sense of Humor and Causes of Mortality: The Nord-Trøndelag Health Study," *Psychosomatic Medicine* 78(3), 2016, 345–53.

Chapter 3: The Anatomy of Funny

80 **the *priming effect*:** J. A. Bargh and T. L. Chartrand, "Studying the Mind in the Middle: A Practical Guide to Priming and Automaticity Research," *Handbook of Research Methods in Social Psychology*, 2000.

80 **laughter's high *emotional contagion*:** J. E. Warren, D. A. Sauter, F. Eisner, J. Wiland, M. A. Dresner, R. J. Wise, . . . and S. K. Scott, "Positive Emotions Preferentially Engage an Auditory-Motor 'Mirror' System," *Journal of Neuroscience* 26(50), 2006, 13067–75.

Chapter 4: Putting Your Funny to Work

102 **the Sapir-Whorf Hypothesis**: P. Kay and W. Kempton, "What Is the Sapir-Whorf Hypothesis?" *American Anthropologist* 86(1), 1984, 65–79.

102 **remote work is on the rise**: W. Johnson, "Leading Remotely," *MIT Sloan Management Review*, winter 2020, https://sloanreview.mit.edu /article/leading-remotely/.

106 **Today's average employee**: M. Chui, J. Manyika, J. Bughin, R. Dobbs, C. Roxburgh, H. Sarrazin, G. Sands, and M. Westergren, "The Social Economy: Unlocking Value and Productivity Through Social Technologies," McKinsey Global Institute, July 2012, https://www.mckinsey .com/industries/technology-media-and-telecommunications/our -insights/the-social-economy.

108 **90 percent of people read the postscript**: S. Vögele, *Handbook of Direct Mail: The Dialogue Method of Direct Written Sales Communication* (Prentice Hall, 1992).

111 **their ratings lined up**: N. Ambady and R. Rosenthal, "Half a Minute: Predicting Teacher Evaluations from Thin Slices of Nonverbal Behavior and Physical Attractiveness," *Journal of Personality and Social Psychology* 64(3), 1993, 431.

112 **Billy Gene Shaw prepared for his first meeting with John**: D. John, *Powershift: Transform Any Situation, Close Any Deal, and Achieve Any Outcome* (Currency, 2020).

120 **Peak-End Rule**: D. Kahneman, B. L. Fredrickson, C. A. Schreiber, and D. A. Redelmeier, "When More Pain Is Preferred to Less: Adding a Better End," *Psychological Science* 4(6), 1993, 401–405.

Chapter 5: Leading with Humor

142 **more than their own boss**: D. Sturt and T. Nordstrum, "10 Shocking Workplace Stats You Need to Know," *Forbes*, March 8, 2018, https:// www.forbes.com/sites/davidsturt/2018/03/08/10-shocking-workplace -stats-you-need-to-know/#76e360b2f3af.

143 **the single biggest issue impacting their performance at work**: J. Morgan, "Trust in the Workplace: What Happened to It, and How Do We Get It Back?" *Forbes*, September 11, 2014.

143 **this crisis in confidence is a threat**: "Redefining Business Success in a Changing World: CEO Survey," PricewaterhouseCoopers, January 2016,

https://www.pwc.com/gx/en/ceo-survey/2016/landing-page/pwc
-19th-annual-global-ceo-survey.pdf.

143 **among the thirty-to-forty-nine demographic**: L. Rainie, S. Keeter, and A. Perrin, "Trust and Distrust in America," Pew Research Center, July 22, 2019.

143 **the percentage of Americans who own dogs**: F. Newport, J. Jones, L. Saad, and J. Carroll, "Americans and Their Pets," Gallup News Service, December 21, 2016.

143 **employees who work in high-trust environments**: 2016 HOW Report. A Global, Empirical Analysis of How Governance, Culture and Leadership Impact Performance.

144 **told a consistent story**: 2019 Edelman Trust Barometer Global Report, https://www.edelman.com/sites/g/files/aatuss191/files/2019-02/2019_Edelman_Trust_Barometer_Global_Report.pdf.

146 **"get away from their manager"**: J. Harter and A. Adkins, "Employees Want a Lot More from Their Managers," *Gallup Workplace*, April 8, 2015.

146 **employee turnover has increased 88 percent**: 2019 Retention Report, Work Institute, https://info.workinstitute.com/hubfs/2019%20Retention%20Report/Work%20Institute%202019%20Retention%20Report%20final-1.pdf.

150 **nearly half of S&P 500 companies will be replaced**: Scott D. Anthony, S. Patrick Viguerie, Evan I. Schwartz, and John Van Landeghem, "2018 Corporate Longevity Forecast: Creative Destruction Is Accelerating," Innosight Insights, https://www.innosight.com/insight/creative-destruction/.

152 **"Laughter serves leaders"**: Dana Bilksy Asher, "The Surprising Link Between Laughter and Learning," *Fast Company*, May 10, 2016.

153 **people who interpret stories from their lives**: Emerging research at Stanford suggests that people who interpret stories from their lives, both positive and negative, as comedies rather than as tragedies or dramas report feeling less stressed and more energetic, challenged, and fulfilled.

158 **an approachable manager**: J. Harter and A. Adkins, "Employees Want a Lot More from Their Managers," *Gallup Workplace*, April 8, 2015.

158 **leaders who use self-deprecating humor**: C. Hoption, J. Barling, and N. Turner, "'It's Not You, It's Me': Transformational Leadership and Self-Deprecating Humor," *Leadership and Organization Development Journal* 34(1), 2013, 4–19. doi: 10.1108/01437731311289947.

161 **"lack of appreciation"**: "Performance Accelerated: A New Benchmark for Initiating Employee Engagement, Retention and Results," OC Tanner Learning Group, https://www.octanner.com/content/dam/oc-tanner/documents/global-research/White_Paper_Performance_Accelerated.pdf.

Chapter 6: Creating a Culture of Levity

170 **more functional communication and problem-solving behaviors**: N. Lehmann-Willenbrock and J. A. Allen, "How Fun Are Your Meetings? Investigating the Relationship Between Humor Patterns in Team Interactions and Team Performance," *Journal of Applied Psychology* 99(6), 2014, 1278.

171 **leaders have a disproportionate influence on organizational culture**: S. Oreg and Y. Berson, "The Impact of Top Leaders' Personalities: The Processes Through Which Organizations Become Reflections of Their Leaders," *Current Directions in Psychological Science* 27(4), 2018, 241–48.

175 **author of—wait for it—*Yes, And.***: K. Leonard, *Yes, And: How Improvisation Reverses "No, But" Thinking and Improves Creativity and Collaboration—Lessons from The Second City* (Harper Business, 2015).

184 **Peak-End Rule**: D. Kahneman, B. L. Frederickson, C. A. Schreiber, and D. A. Redelmeier, "When More Pain Is Preferred to Less: Adding a Better End," *Psychological Science* 4(6), 1993, 401–405.

187 **a source of group cohesion**: F. Gino and M. I. Norton, "Why Rituals Work," *Scientific American*, May 14, 2013.

189 **the "primal mark"**: J. M. Berg, "The Primal Mark: How the Beginning Shapes the End in the Development of Creative Ideas," *Organizational Behavior and Human Decision Processes* 125(1), 2014, 1–17.

Chapter 7: Navigating the Gray Areas of Humor

209 **making you more relatable and approachable**: A. Gherini, "What a Self-Deprecating Sense of Humor Says About Your EQ," *Inc.*, November 29, 2018.

209 **when people of lower status self-deprecate**: T. B. Bitterly, A. W. Brooks, and M. E. Schweitzer, "Risky Business: When Humor Increases and Decreases Status," *Journal of Personality and Social Psychology* 112(3), 2017, 431–55.

210 more likely to elicit laughter when delivered to "subordinates": T. F. Stillman, R. F. Baumeister, and C. Nathan DeWall, "What's So Funny About Not Having Money? The Effects of Power on Laughter," *Personality and Social Psychology Bulletin* 33(11), 2007, 1547–58.

211 those who believed the joke teller to be higher status: Ibid.

214 that the recipient would interpret that tone accurately: J. Kruger, N. Epley, J. Parker, and Z. W. Ng, "Egocentrism over E-mail: Can We Communicate as Well as We Think?" *Journal of Personality and Social Psychology* 89(6), 2005, 925.

218 greater tolerance of gender harassment: R. K. Mallett, T. E. Ford, and J. A. Woodzicka, "What Did He Mean by That? Humor Decreases Attributions of Sexism and Confrontation of Sexist Jokes," *Sex Roles* 75 (5–6), 2016, 272–84.

218 recommended bigger funding cuts to a women's organization: T. E. Ford, C. F. Boxer, J. Armstrong, and J. R. Edel, "More than 'Just a Joke': The Prejudice-Releasing Function of Sexist Humor," *Personality and Social Psychology Bulletin* 34(2), 2008, 159–70.

INDEX

DR. JENNIFER AAKER is the General Atlantic Professor at Stanford Graduate School of Business. A behavioral scientist and author, Dr. Aaker is a leading expert on how purpose and meaning shape the choices individuals make, how money and time can be used in ways that cultivate long-lasting happiness, and how technology can positively impact human well-being. Dr. Aaker is widely published in leading scholarly journals and her work has been featured in *The Economist, The New York Times, The Wall Street Journal, The Atlantic,* and *Science.* Dr. Aaker co-authored the award-winning book *The Dragonfly Effect,* and is the recipient of the Distinguished Scientific Achievement Award, Stanford Distinguished Teaching Award, and the MBA Professor of the Year Award. At Stanford, she teaches classes including Designing AI to Cultivate Human Well-Being, Rethinking Purpose, A New Type of Leader, VR/AR: Scaling Empathy in an Immersive World, Power of Story, and Humor: Serious Business. Dr. Aaker serves as a board member and adviser helping companies and leadership teams with digital transformation, global brand building, and embracing a new type of leadership for the innovation economy—one anchored on purpose, fueled by levity. Personally, she counts winning a dance-off in the early 1980s among her most impressive feats; and her abbreviated cooking skills have earned her family Doordash Platinum status.

NAOMI BAGDONAS is a lecturer at the Stanford Graduate School of Business and an executive coach. She runs a strategy consultancy
designing and facilitating intentional, interac-
tive sessions for the leadership teams, boards,
and partners of Fortune 100 companies. Leaders turn to Naomi in moments of personal and
organizational change to help them unlock
creativity and innovation, dissolve barriers to
progress, and create lasting impact for their
cultures and businesses. Versed in humor, behavioral science, and human perceptions,
Naomi coaches executives and celebrities for
media appearances ranging from *Saturday*
Night Live to the *Today* show, as well as for high-profile speaking engage-
ments. When she was at Deloitte, Naomi helped create Business Chemistry,
a system that enables people to collaborate more effectively across different
working styles, and that over 500,000 people around the world have used to
build stronger relationships and higher-performing teams. Formally trained
at the Upright Citizens Brigade Theatre, Naomi performs at comedy venues,
sharing how life's absurdities are common experiences connecting us. She
also teaches improv comedy for resilience in San Francisco's county jail.
Naomi fosters a constant stream of rescue dogs who provide boundless love
and comic relief while destroying everything she owns.

Humorseriously.com